MAKING IT IN MUSIC

This is the inside story about how the music industry really works, about the people who make the records and manage the artists, organise the publicity and the gigs, run the tours and sell the albums, in the words of those people themselves.

Discover how they started in the business, what their jobs are really like, what you need to make it and how to make a start yourself; there's even a complete list of music courses.

A fascinating insight into the music industry and essential reading for the career-minded.

MAKING IT IN MUSIC

JOHN PIDGEON

KNIGHT BOOKS
Hodder and Stoughton

The right of John Pidgeon to be identified as the author of this work has been asserted by him in accordance with the Copyright, Designs and Patents Act 1988.

Printed and bound in Great Britain for Hodder and Stoughton Chil-dren's Books, a division of Hodder and Stoughton Ltd, Mill Road, Dunton Green, Sevenoaks, Kent TN13 2YA. (Editorial Office: 47 Bedford Square, London WC1B 3DP) by Cox & Wyman Ltd, Read-ing, Berks. Photoset by Rowland Phototypesetting Ltd, Bury St Ed-munds, Suffolk.

British Library C.I.P.

Pidgeon, John
  Making it in music.
  I. Title
  780.68

ISBN 0-340-53682-9

Contents

Introduction

The music business is an enormous industry, incorporating a variety of careers. The one thing – in many instances the only thing – that connects those careers is the music itself. Whatever else you need to make it in music, a love of music is a must.

The music business has grown with each new musical explosion since rock 'n' roll arrived like a tidal wave from America in the mid-fifties. It grew with the Beatles and the beat groups boom, with rhythm and blues, with soul music and psychedelia in the sixties; it grew with teenybop pop, with glitter rock and glam rock, with supergroups, punk rock, reggae and disco in the seventies; it grew with synthesizers, samplers, rappers, scratchers and dancers, with heavy metal and with world music in the eighties; and it continues to grow with everything that's gone before and more in the nineties.

Many of the people in music have grown with the business. They came into it from different directions and followed different routes to reach where they are today. They learned what they know from those around them, and from their own successes and mistakes. Often there was no other way to learn. There were no college courses. Record producers started out as tea boys, record company executives as sales reps or secretaries, managers by running college dances, whatever it took to find a way in.

Making It In Music is not a conventional careers guide. Nor is it a handbook to the music business. It won't tell you how to qualify in A&R or publishing or PR, because, apart from the conventional standards required in legal and accountancy departments, there are no qualifications that guarantee a career in the music business. In music, perhaps more than any other industry, employers are less interested in a certificate than the person it has been awarded to.

What *Making It In Music* does is tell you, in the words of people who have made it themselves, what worked for them: what they did at school, and between school and moving into the music business, how they got their start, how they worked their way up, what that work entailed, the good times and bad times, the dos and don'ts, the qualities it took to get them where they are, and the qualities you will need if you, like them, want to make it in music.

I should like to thank the following for being so generous with their time, advice and experience: Keith Altham (independent publicist/Keith Altham Publicity); Lisa Anderson (former managing director/RCA Records); Ed Bicknell (manager/Dire Straits); Pete Buckland (tour manager/Rod Stewart, Paul Young, etc); Dennis Collopy (managing director/Big Life Music); Paul Conroy (president/Chrysalis Records International); Paul Curran (managing director/BMG Music Publishing); Neil Ferris (independent record promoter/Ferret 'n' Spanner Plugging Company and PR); Malcolm Hill (general manager of promotion/Capitol/Parlophone Records); Max Hole (managing director/East West Records); Paul King (concert promoter and manager/Tears For Fears); Chris Lamb (tour production manager/Madonna, Paul McCartney, etc); Pat 'Boiler' Logue (road manager/Def Leppard, Rod Stewart, etc); Graham Lyle (songwriter/Michael Jackson, Tina Turner, etc); Ian McLagan (musician/Rolling Stones, Bruce Springsteen, Rod Stewart, etc); Jonathan Morrish (director of corporate press and PR/Sony Music); Hugh Padgham (record producer and engineer/Phil Collins, Julia Fordham, Sting, etc); Tony Powell (managing director/MCA Records); Tim Renwick (musician/Eric Clapton, Elton John, Pink Floyd, etc); Jill Sinclair (managing director/Sarm Studios and ZTT Records); Nigel Sweeney (independent record promoter/Ferret 'n' Spanner Plugging Company and PR).

MAKING a START in MUSIC

KEITH ALTHAM,
PUBLICIST

Education: commercial college (O levels, including shorthand and typing, and A levels). First job: journalist on sports monthly; then pop magazine Fabulous *before joining* New Musical Express; *left to freelance for* Melody Maker *and other publications.*

A friend of mine said, would I like to do some PR (public relations) for his band? I said, no, I didn't want to be a PR – dreadful people. I'd spent nine years of my life avoiding PRs as a journalist and trying to beat down the walls between them and the artist. But eventually I succumbed, because he said to me, 'Look, there's an office, a typewriter and a phone, none of which you have to pay for. All you've got to do is make a few phone calls for the group and I'll pay you for that.' So I took it, and the first thing I had to look after was a No 1, so it just became a question of picking up the phone and making arrangements to set up interviews, and I was beginning to think that PR was a piece of cake, which it isn't. In fact, I wasn't really that daft, I knew I was lucky with the particular thing that I was doing.

Anyway, what happened then was that a lot of people that I'd been doing journalistic work with, rang me up and said, now that I was doing PR, was I interested in representing them? And at first I said no, because I wanted to carry on being a freelance journalist, and the PR was more of a sideline than anything else, and then I thought, 'Well, this is stupid. I'm turning down a lot of money and I need to also take care of the home front,' so I went to see a friend of mine, who had been in PR for about three years, and said, 'Look, I've been offered all this work, I'm not really an experienced PR, I don't have the contacts and background, to do it I need to work with somebody who has, and we'll split it,' which is what we did.

LISA ANDERSON,
FORMER MANAGING DIRECTOR RCA
RECORDS

Education: public school (O levels); finishing school in Switzerland, 'which actually served me to good purpose, as it turned out in the end, because I learned to speak French'; secretarial college. First job: secretary – 'I worked for the same chap for about two years and then decided all of this was really rather boring, and by chance, literally by chance, got a job working in the music business.'

I loved music the same as everybody else does when you're that sort of age, and quite by chance I got into a pretty dodgy film music company, and I worked there for about three or four months until it closed itself down, but then got offered various other jobs through the people I'd met there, and eventually ended up working for Chrysalis Records, a fairly large independent company which covered a lot of bases. It was obviously a record company, publishing company, it owned the Rainbow Theatre at the time, it had an agency, it was quite an all-round independent record company, and I worked for the managing director as his secretary.

And so I got to learn quite a lot of different things, especially because he was a manager as well, so I would get involved with the nitty gritty of putting a tour together, the paperwork, that sort of thing. I learned a lot. Secretary is a very undervalued position altogether, because you get to know everything that your boss is doing. There is more to be learned from it than many people would like to think. I did that for about two years.

ED BICKNELL,
ARTIST MANAGER

Education: grammar school (O levels – 'I miserably failed Mathematics, which is funny, because that's what I do a lot of' – and A levels); university – 'I ran the folk club, the jazz club, became social secretary . . . through that I got to know quite a lot of people in the agency business' – (BA Social Studies). First job: booking agent – 'I wanted to be a professional drummer. I came to London and ended up in what became the Average White Band, who then were called

Mogul Thrash, and I got fired for not being Scottish. They wanted an all-Scottish group.'

I was walking down Oxford Street literally the next day, and I happened to bump into a guy who was one of the agents I'd dealt with, and I said to him, 'I haven't got a job, I've just been fired from the group,' and he said those immortal words which any readers will probably hear if they go into music: 'I can't pay you anything, but why don't you come and work for us and you can have half of everything you earn for the office?' The result of that was that in the year of 1970 I submitted a tax return for a gross income of £74 and in 1971 that went up to £138, numbers that are tattooed on my brain.

Dire Straits were the most commercial band worldwide of the whole of the eighties in record-selling terms and they've sold about sixty-five million albums since we started, but I had no idea when I met them that that would happen and I had no desire that it would happen. I didn't look at it from a financial point of view or a glory point of view or an ego point of view. I walked into Dingwalls (a London club) and I thought, 'Oh, I really like these songs, and I think this guitarist's really good,' and he had a red Stratocaster, which reminded me of the Shadows. That was what made the most impact on me that evening. I didn't see £ signs zipping in front of my head.

The preceding week a friend of mine in the A&R (artists and repertoire) department had called me up and he'd said, 'I've just signed this band called Dire Straits. Would you be their agent?' And I had a tour coming up with Talking Heads, in January 1978, and I needed an opening act, and because I happened to like this chap who called me, I acceded to his request to go and see this group at Dingwalls the following Tuesday – December 13th 1977 – and we went out to dinner and I walked in and they were playing what, in fact, became the first album, and I really liked them.

Anyway, I nipped into the dressing room at the end of the evening, said hello, knocked Mark's (Knopfler) guitar over as I walked in, invited them to come into the agency office the next day, and three of the four of them duly came in. We had a brief chat, I offered them the Talking Heads tour – twenty-three gigs in twenty-six days, £50 a night, they could ride in the Talking Heads' bus, eat the Talking Heads' food, use the Talking Heads' PA and lights. I would slip the Talking Heads' sound man a fiver every night to do the sound, which I did. The band would stay in one hotel room, two to a double bed.

And we had a general chat and I said I'd really like to manage them, and I think it's important to note here that I had never managed anybody at that time. I didn't know what it meant. What I knew was that I could get them gigs, because that was what I was doing, and I also knew from the managers that we were dealing with in the office that the standard of management was truly abysmal. Anyway, Mark rang me back the next day, and he said, 'Yes, we'd like to do this tour,' and it was very much a question of 'Do you have a van?' 'No.' 'Have you got any roadies?' 'Well, we've got one.' 'Have you got any money?' 'No.'

PETE BUCKLAND,
TOUR MANAGER

Education: comprehensive school (RSAs); day release college (City & Guilds). First job: precision engineer.

I was helping Aynsley Dunbar (drummer/leader of Aynsley Dunbar Retaliation) out on a part-time basis, and going off on my holidays doing continental tours and stuff. I got to know the Who's guys very well, as a result of always going to their shows and just being around – I think Aynsley supported them on a couple of occasions – and Ronnie Lane (Faces bass player) had asked them if they knew of anyone who would be suitable for looking after them. Ronnie rang me up in April or May 1969 to ask me if I would be interested in a job for this new band that was being formed out of the old Small Faces and half of the Jeff Beck Group, and I said yes. He said it was happening at some stage and he'd let me know when. I got a call from him in September, saying that it was imminent, and I went round to meet with the boys at (Faces manager) Billy Gaff's place for an interview, the highlight of which was all the boys on Gaff's couch pushing the couch over backwards and rolling over with their legs in the air. We all went off and had a drink and that was it. I handed in my notice at work.

DENNIS COLLOPY,
MANAGING DIRECTOR
BIG LIFE MUSIC

Education: O and A levels; university – 'the night before I gradu-ated, I said, "The only thing I can honestly think of myself doing is something to do with music"' – (BA German) First job: computer programmer – 'I found I really had an affinity for that, I really liked what I was doing, but I hated the people I was working with, who were really boring.'

I walked into Reeds Employment Agency in Oxford Circus, and I was by this time desperate, I really just wanted a job in London, almost anything would do. And I put my interests – music, all of the stuff you put down on application forms, but mainly music – and what my qualifications were. I was honest. And this girl just said, 'I've got a job here in the copyright department at Chrysler Records.' I said. 'Well, I'll go for that,' and she said, 'Okay, I'll arrange an interview – this is the address,' and she wrote it out as Chrysler Records. And of course I knew enough about the music business to know it had to be Chrysalis Records.

So I went along for the interview and it turned out to be the music publishing company. They had a real vibe at Chrysalis, all the directors of the company had degrees, so I couldn't have walked into a better company with a degree. They were quite proud. It was like showing off your pet. 'Hey, here he comes, you know, we've got a graduate working in the copyright department.'

Every contract they'd ever signed I précised. And I worked from ten till about eight every night, and I just tried to absorb knowledge as much as possible. I had no real preconceptions. I didn't really know where I was going, except I was happy in what I was doing. I was dealing with music.

I had a boss who was very taken with the fact that he had a graduate, and he was very taken with the notion of educating me about the business and treating it as a subject. He was a really nice man and he actually said, 'Okay, I'll teach you everything I know,' and he did. And it stuck. Obviously by having been reasonably well educated, I knew how to pick up knowledge fairly quickly and store it, and apparently Chrysalis still use my précis of all their contracts.

PAUL CONROY,
PRESIDENT CHRYSALIS RECORDS INTERNATIONAL

Education: technical college (O and A levels); teacher training college. First job: booking agent – 'When I was social secretary at college, I never thought, "Oh, it's showbiz for me." I really stumbled into the music business by being a social sec. I suppose I could've been a teacher. My parents would've much preferred me to have gone into something which would have given me a pension and a lifelong job. I did a year's teacher's training and I thought, "This is all a bit dull," so I decided to give it a crack and started for £17 a week, and in the first couple of days you realised it was a hard slog.'

I was for a number of years an agent, and I then got involved with a bunch of lads called the Kursaal Flyers, who I managed for quite a few years, and then in about '76 I was dragged screaming into Stiff Records and was general manager there for quite a number of years, and then I had seven years at WEA, where I was managing director of the US division, and now I'm the president of Chrysalis Records International for the world excluding North America.

PAUL CURRAN,
MANAGING DIRECTOR BMG MUSIC PUBLISHING

Education: O and A levels; university (BA Spanish). First job: music publishing – 'at the very bottom of the ladder.'

While I was at university I was in bands and I was in theatre groups and I did a couple of shows at the Edinburgh Festival and then came to London with songs that I'd written for that to try and get the ball rolling. I was thinking of going round record companies with tapes, saying, 'Here's a show I've just done in Edinburgh, do you want to take it on?' being a bit naive, and somebody then said, 'You should go and see a music publisher,' which I started to do. And I met a few publishers and had a few rebuttals and ended up finding a supporter who was prepared to help me demo new songs and was trying to help me place my songs as a songwriter.

I suppose six months on from doing that, I was told that there was a temporary job going at Chappell, a summer vacancy, which I went along for, and I got that. That was basically my start, and from there that temp job became a full-time opportunity.

It was the sheet music library with all the shows and all the songs – pop and standard, as they say – and it was an interesting place to start in publishing, because everybody in the building at some point had a point of contact in the library, and obviously knowledge of the catalogue and how it was being worked, it was a free education.

From there I then progressed up through the standard side to the pop side, signing bands, signing writers, working with writers, plugging songs, in a big company. It was not as big as it had been, but it was certainly a much bigger publishing house than we see anywhere now in terms of creative staff. There were five or six people working in different areas, be it bands, songwriters, shows on the standard side, and it was a free education really, and I don't think there are many places where you get that free education any more, because publishing is now a much sleeker machine.

NEIL FERRIS,
INDEPENDENT RECORD PROMOTER

Education: O and A levels – 'Whilst I was doing my O levels and A levels I really got involved in local radio, and by the time I finished school I was offered a place at the Central London Poly, a degree course in Broadcasting and Journalism, which I decided to turn down, because at that time the BBC wasn't accepting it as an entrance into the BBC full-time.' First job: local radio producer and presenter – 'I produced loads and loads of local radio programmes, and produced a few documentaries for Radio 4, and I just got fed up with the BBC, and went into the record business. I just fell into it.'

Somebody who was asking me to play their records on programmes I was producing, said, 'Why don't you think about going into the record business?' And I met this woman in Brighton who ran Francis, Day & Hunter, the music publishers. She knew my parents and she said, 'Why don't you come and work for me? I'll pay you thirty quid a week.'

I was a junior in the promotion department, but that was easy, because I was going up to Radio 1, seeing people at Radio 1, talking to them about records, and I already knew them, because I'd been making trails and stuff at Brighton for Radio 1. So it was like really weird. I was talking to people who I either knew or who knew of me or I knew of them.

It's a horrible thing working for a music publisher, because the record companies don't really want you going into radio and TV people talking about their records, because they're the record company and they look down their nose at people who work for publishers, but publishing promotion is really important, because you're representing the writer and you're interested in the writer's work. But anyway, I worked for them for a while, and then moved on to a record company, which was real promotion.

MALCOLM HILL,
HEAD OF PROMOTIONS CAPITOL/
PARLOPHONE RECORDS

Education: grammar school (O levels); art college – 'I learned how to back horses. I can't remember what I did there.' First jobs: disc jockey – 'I was resident disc jockey at Bury Football Club for quite a long time and I had a mobile disco as well, so that's where the music involvement started – I think from 18 to 20 I was more or less a professional disc jockey in the Manchester area, I can't remember doing much other work; I had a couple of little excursions into radio with BBC Radio Manchester and a little bit when Piccadilly started up, nothing very serious'; childrenswear showroom manager; trainee works manager; breathing equipment salesman; bedding factory manager – 'I remember doing Christmas discos for all these old ladies in the canteen, it was very, very funny.'

The big break came when I was twenty-four. The guy who ran this factory that made bedspreads, quilts and eiderdowns was reading *The Guardian* one day and he said, 'Oh yeah, you like music. EMI are advertising for junior sales reps.' Well, at twenty-four I wasn't exactly junior, but it was a way in there, and he was really pissed off, because I got the job. He even offered to make me a partner in the business, but bedspreads, quilts and eiderdowns wasn't exactly what I wanted to do. And that's when I joined EMI, when I was twenty-four, as a junior salesman. I thought it was brilliant, because I was still messing about in a little Escort van that had all my disco equipment, and EMI gave me a company car.

My area was everywhere north of Birmingham to Scotland, and I stayed away and just lived in the car for a year. It was brilliant. I was away three or four weeks at a time.

About a year and a half later I got my own area, then an opening came up. EMI decided to split the company into two and split the sales force, and basically left me without a job, but they knew I wanted to get into promotions, so I was found a job working out of the regional promotion office in Manchester, then they moved me down to Birmingham, doing BRMB, Beacon, Trent, BBC Leicester.

It was really exciting. All these stations were opening up and we were trying to make something of the regional radio stations and worked very closely with them.

Most of all I can remember working with touring acts. Every time you had an act come through the city you'd ship them all round the Midlands to every station, try to fix up interviews for them all over the place. I can remember working on six shows one night, which included Elton John and Cliff Richard, being at each show and doing interviews at each show with various artists.

MAX HOLE,
MANAGING DIRECTOR EAST WEST RECORDS

Education: public school (O and A levels); university — 'Within a few weeks I ran the folk club, I had a radio programme twice a week on the campus radio station, and I was social secretary. I didn't study much law, but I studied quite a lot of music business. I was also managing the university group, and the first deal I ever negotiated was when I went to the university and I said, "We want to take a sabbatical year off." My dad went mental, couldn't believe the tax-payers' money was going to be spent on something so worthless, and I never went back.' First job: booking agent.

Through booking all the groups for the university dances, I met a guy who was a booker, and he wanted to start an agency of his own and asked me if I wanted to go and work there. From agency we got involved in management, and then we had a production company. I got involved in managing producers, and I also managed a group called the Inmates. They were with WEA, and the then managing director and head of A&R asked me if I'd like to go for lunch one day, and I assumed they wanted to talk to me about the Inmates, and they suddenly said, 'Oh no, we don't want to talk to you about the Inmates, we'd like you to come and be an A&R man.' And I went, 'Ooh, no, I don't want to be an A&R man. They're those horrible people you can't get on the phone. They never do anything and they're all deaf.'

I also had a record label called Criminal Records — 'the label you can't trust' — which did okay, but it was always a bit of a struggle, and I thought, well, yeah, it might be interesting actually to work within a major record company. And I agreed with them that I could still manage the three record producers who I managed, partly because I think they'd never heard of them at that stage, and I took the job.

PAUL KING,
ARTIST MANAGER AND CONCERT PROMOTER

Education: O and A levels; university – 'I was what they call a social sec, and in fact I was social sec for three years as opposed to one year, and I managed to get my degree at the same time by default' – (Bsc Nuclear Chemistry). First job: booking agent.

Most of the people that came out of university went the agency route, because that was the easiest way. What you basically did was you agreed to work for no money, a lot of them worked on commission, so unless you booked dates, you didn't earn any money. So it was quite easy to get a job, because the person that you worked for didn't actually have to fork out any money until you made some money, but at least it was a stepping stone, you slowly built up your contacts.

You're cossetted really in university. Your audience is there already, you don't have to go and find them. As long as you put the sign up in the lav, they turn up at the concert, but when you're out in the real world, you've got to put posters up on the street and put ads in the paper and all that sort of stuff, and at university if you lose money no one asks any questions, or they certainly don't ask serious questions, so it's toy town, it really is toy town. I spent two years learning how to do it for real and then I started up on my own.

I'd always wanted to be my own boss anyway, so I actually went home and put a couple of phone lines in the house and I retained the sole booking of the Rock Garden (London club) and I took a couple of the bands with me, and I booked them for the first couple of years and it paid me a decent living wage.

CHRIS LAMB,
TOUR PRODUCTION MANAGER

Education: 'Looking back there are things I wish I'd learned or knew more about when I was in school. Every little thing you can learn in school is really important, because it can help you in your life if you want it to.' First job: US Navy electrician.

I never planned on getting into this business. I didn't know anything about music. I went into the military – Vietnam and all of that – and when I got out of the navy and started looking for work, I ran into some guy who was using old navy searchlights for a rock show. I knew how to work them, because I'd learned how to build them in the navy, and I started working on lights for rock shows. And I've been touring round the world ever since then in different capacities. I used to do lighting and I drove trucks and built outdoor stages. I did just about anything anybody asked me to do.

PAT 'BOILER' LOGUE,
ROAD MANAGER

Education: left school at 16. First job: apprentice electrician – 'I was also putting up neon signs, and a lot of restaurants had to be done when they were closed, so you'd do a day's work, then go to a restaurant at midnight when it was closed and work till four in the morning. I was earning a hundred pounds a week, getting treble money, and I gave up a hundred quid a week for thirty quid, but it was treble the fun though.'

My best friend was a guitar player in a band and they needed help one night, taking them to the gig in my car, that was it, and me being an electrician I was roped in to sort out the wiring, and it went from there. They were called Flesh. I was with them, running them around and whatever, and still working, and then they had a chance to go professional and do an album, so I decided to jack in and stay with them.

I knew nothing then. In those days you just put the amp up and plugged it in and away they went, but all the time I was picking up bits and pieces. As you're dragging equipment up twelve flights to a college and down again, you learn how to lift a cabinet and how to plug it in so it won't blow up halfway through the show, and how many amps to put on one plug top, that sort of stuff.

GRAHAM LYLE,
SONGWRITER

Education: O and A levels. First job: songwriter/musician – 'I said, "Listen, give me a year of trying to write and trying to get somewhere, and if nothing happens, then, okay, I'll look for a straight job."'

My father was terrific. He gave me money to buy two tape recorders, and you could cross the two of them over and make a fair multi-track demo. From that I got my very first cover, and I think the fact that I'd got one was enough to let my father and mother let me go on for a little longer, and it gave me hope also.

The first cover was a case of me sending a tape off to London, and it was like, 'Oh, this sounds good. Come down and see me.' So I went down to London and they asked me to sign this contract, which I knew nothing about. There was no money involved and it probably was scandalous, but I didn't know what I was signing. I signed it anyway, and the idea was I'd send whatever songs I wrote for the next year or so. The contract tied me up totally. He'd send up £25 from time to time, but actually I just kept all the money and sent it all back and said, 'I want out,' and he gave me the contract back, which was great.

At the same time I was involved in a local band, so I would play weekends with the band and during the week I'd try and write my songs. Our band had been getting better and started doing our own songs, and it was that time when A&R guys came up to Scotland looking for the new Scottish Beatles, signing bands up right, left and centre, and they signed our band up. We did one or two records, and one of them came pretty close to being a hit. It got a terrific review – I'll never forget it – and hearing it for the first time on the radio was fantastic. I don't think you ever quite get the same buzz as hearing your own record for the first time on the radio.

By that time Benny Gallagher and I were writing together. We decided that we had to make the move to London, if we were going to be serious about it. When we first came down, we had to have jobs and write at night. I worked for the British Steel Corporation for about a year and then we got the break with Apple (the Beatles' company). That was really the turning point, because they employed us on a nine-to-five, five day a week basis, to write songs. We were only with Apple for about a year, year and a half, but it was good in that we were forced to sit down and come up at the end of the week with a song or two songs, whatever we could do, and also Paul McCartney would set us tasks. He'd say, 'Mary Hopkin's doing a new album – I want you to write a B-side to the single,' or whatever, which was a thing we'd never done before, we'd always written for ourselves or our own band, and it was good for us to have to channel in any one direction.

IAN MCLAGAN,
MUSICIAN

Education: left grammar school at 15 – 'I can't do anything else other than this, and it's not always a means to earning a living – some months are brilliant, others you wonder whether you'll ever work again – I'd get your degree'; art college – 'The still life I did for the entrance exam was band instruments on stage, so I was already into music. I never got my diploma, because as soon as I got there I met up with some other guys and we formed a group, and I went professional from then. The Beatles happened, and the Stones happened right in my neighbourhood, so I left school because I wanted to be one of them, I wanted to play that music.' First job: musician.

When I first got an organ, I saw an ad in the papers: 'Hammond organ, free trial in your own home for two weeks.' I thought I'd have a free trial and use it on gigs, and after two weeks I'd send it back and do the same thing with another firm, but they wouldn't allow me to move it from the house. I had Booker T & the MGs' *Green Onions* album, and I had the organ in the dining-room, and all I'd do was go through the whole album and play through each track until I knew exactly the settings on the organ that Booker T had. That blew my mind and – wallop! – Booker T was the most important thing in my life.

The group fell apart because we couldn't support ourselves, and I joined the Boz People as an organist, whereas before I was just in a band with my mates and I wasn't very good, but it didn't matter so much because we were all learning. I think I was with the Boz People six or nine months, during which time we played a lot and messed around a lot. I was a professional musician, not earning any money, but definitely a professional musician, which made me feel pretty good. I left the group after I realised that nobody was that keen on doing the gigs. It was more of a laugh.

I left on a Saturday and on the Monday morning I got a phone call from (artist manager) Don Arden's office that there was a job available. After a day of wondering what the job was, they introduced me to the Small Faces. That's when I really started working – every night of the week from that very moment.

JONATHAN MORRISH,
DIRECTOR OF CORPORATE PRESS AND PUBLICITY SONY MUSIC

Education: O and A levels; university – 'I left not knowing what the hell I wanted to do' – (BA English). First job: freelance music journalist – 'Once you've got a foot in the door and you know one person, then one person quickly becomes three people, becomes ten, becomes twenty; therefore, once I'd had my first piece published, it wasn't just easier to get another piece published in the same magazine, but also to get other magazines interested.'

I heard through the grapevine that CBS were looking for somebody to come in on a two day a week basis to write all their press releases and biogs. It gave me the chance to see a record company at work, which, when you're writing about music, can be quite a strange, almost intimidating process. I was lucky in that I could see the record company process from both sides of the fence.

After about a year of doing that, I really felt I was going to pursue writing seriously or I was going to get into a record company, and obviously with the sort of contacts that I'd built up, if I was going to get into a record company, then a press office was going to be the likeliest point of entry.

HUGH PADGHAM,
RECORD PRODUCER AND ENGINEER

Education: public school (O and A levels) – 'The school had a tape recorder and we taped our rehearsals sometimes. You can imagine one mike with a band playing, with my bass probably going through an old radio or something, and so I suddenly sort of thought, "I like this tape recorder business," and then I discovered what a studio was through a magazine. It had a section on studios, and I saw these consoles and I thought, "Wow, all these knobs – and recording music," because I'd only really just discovered how the microphone worked and the tape and stuff, I thought, "This is the life for me."'
First job: tape operator.

There weren't that many studios around then, not compared to now, and secondly there was the parents problems, because they would have liked me to have gone to university, having spent all this money on my education, or get a job with the BBC or some sort of proper organisation rather than me say I wanted to start as a tea boy. So I decided much against my parents' wishes that I was definitely going to do this, and I said, 'Don't worry, I will succeed.'

There really were so few top studios in London, maybe twenty at the very most, and this magazine just had a list of them. So I just wrote to them all.

I actually wasn't a total tea boy, but I started off at Advision studios in London as a sort of tea boy-cum-tape op on eleven or twelve quid a week, and I'm terribly thankful to my parents now, because without their support I don't know how I could have survived, because I didn't live in London, so I had to have a flat, which was I think ten quid a week, and then the cost of getting to and from the studio on public transport – and if you worked late they only paid two pounds fifty and the taxi used to cost four quid, so you were down whichever way you looked – so luckily for me my parents supported me to an extent that I could live.

I guess I was a bit of a pompous public schoolboy in a way, and I remember them saying, 'You've got to learn all the microphones.' There were hundreds of microphones and I thought, 'No, I don't need to learn the names of the microphones, I'll just look at them and know it,' which I didn't. But it was weird. I think people are much better now in studios, but I felt in those days that the tape op was the person who the engineer could really bully, you know, a bit like at school, and I was scared to death for a good couple of months, I suppose, and the thing was, some people were good at answering questions that you asked, but it seemed like in a way, 'Well, if I tell you my secrets, you're going to nick my gig,' sort of thing, so I got the feeling that a lot of people weren't into telling me things.

I only stayed there about six months because, supposedly because of the economic climate, they decided they couldn't afford to have me, so they made me redundant, but I think it's because I was pretty useless actually.

TONY POWELL,
MANAGING DIRECTOR MCA RECORDS

Education: left school at 16 – 'My father was a butcher, and I was the one who was designated to follow in his footsteps, so I really didn't bother at school. I enjoyed my swimming and my games and being a hooligan and hanging out in coffee bars and the only qualification I had was one O level in Maths – and I struggled to get that, I think.'
First jobs: butcher – 'Unfortunately my father died after about a year and that was me left out on a limb, so I was on the dole for about six months, struggling around, doing a bit of painting and decorating, stuff like that, but underneath all of this I'd always loved music'; club manager – 'There was a guy opening a sort of disco where I came from, and I went along there and said, "Are there any jobs going?" And they said, "Yeah, if you want to help behind the bar." Well, within about a week I'd become in charge of the bar and also become assistant manager. Through the doors over a period of a year and a half, two years, I think I saw every major name with the exception of the Beatles, which allowed me to form great relationships with a lot of different people, and that stood me in great stead for the future career.'

I stayed in the club business for a good three or four more years, transferring from basically a dance/disco to a proper night club up in Manchester, but that didn't seem to work out – there was always the longing for the pop side – and I left and was desperate to get in the record business and, as most people find nowadays, even with contacts, trying to get in the record business is very, very hard.

I had this huge list of people I'd got to know, and I started ringing them: 'Any jobs? Any jobs? Any jobs?' And it was all: 'No, sorry. No, sorry. No, sorry.' And a friend of mine, who'd helped me at the club, worked for a record company and he was a sort of salesman, and he said that this company was starting up a separate operation selling budget records. You had a van full of records and you went to sweet shops and newsagents, anybody that you could con into taking two hundred records, and the idea was that, if they didn't sell them, you would exchange them for some new ones next month.

So I thought, 'Well, I'll try this – at least I'm in the record business.' And I was very lucky. It was very early days and a lot of people seemed to want these cheap records. I was on commission and the guy who had set it up hadn't done his sums properly and I was earning far more commission than I should have done, and they swiftly said, 'This guy's doing pretty good here. We've got a proper salesman's job for him with a car in Nottingham. We'll transfer him there.'

So I started ploughing my way round record shops on a monthly selling cycle, which is still done nowadays, selling the records that were about to come out. And I seemed to do pretty well at that and became area manager as well. I had some people working under me, which allowed me to learn a few man-management skills, but while doing that, of course, I was still in contact with the artists, and one of the artists that I got to know was Rod Stewart.

I used to see him from time to time when he turned up at one or two of the venues. He'd had success in America with his second album, *Gasoline Alley*, and was having horrendous problems with the record company people in London, who didn't seem to understand him. Rod was signed to the American associate of our company, and the president of that company was phoning and giving the company president in England a lot of gyp, saying, 'This act is going to be massive in America. You've got to look after my artist. The only person who seems to understand this artist is a salesman up in the Midlands somewhere.' And I got this phone call from the chairman one night, saying, 'Get down to London. I want to see you in the morning.' I got down, thinking I was going to get the sack because I'd said something out of place, and I was given this job to do artist relations.

After a couple of years of roaming around the world with Rod – I had some fun along the way, plenty of drinking, being on his album sleeves! – I thought, 'I'm going to make a good career of this.' And so I really set about then deciding the areas I wanted to go into, and I wasn't quite sure, but having had the selling background, I thought maybe marketing was an interesting thing.

TIM RENWICK,
MUSICIAN

Education: 'removed' from school at 14 – 'I started playing the guitar when I was 14, so it sort of merged with my education and I lost interest really and wanted to play in a band'; technical colleges (two O levels and a 'half-hearted attempt' at a Hotel Management course) – 'In fact, it was bloody hard work, so I thought, "No, this isn't for me," and started in earnest with bands.' First job: musician.

I started playing the clarinet when I was ten, and I did quite well at that, but everything tends to be loaded with snobbery, and turning up with jeans and long hair wasn't the done thing, so I rejected that and started playing in bands, a couple of dreadful local bands, and then I joined a fairly established semi-pro band, playing four or five nights a week and earning some money at last.

We rented a house for the band to live in, so you could live fairly cheaply, and I suppose at the time I was probably ending up with fifteen, twenty quid a week, which at the time was quite a wedge. You'd go through all the general discomforts of being in a budding band, like every time you go to Wales the van breaks down and you spend the night at the side of the road, sleeping on the Hammond organ, all that sort of stuff, over and over again. We'd basically go anywhere. We'd go to Aberdeen for twenty-five quid. It was: there's a gig. Right, get in the van. No questions. Boom. We'd do it.

Eventually we decided that the only thing to do was to move to London, so we did for a while, and that kind of foundered, and I eventually ended up living in Notting Hill Gate by myself, and that was when Quiver started up. We did a couple of albums, but we always had trouble writing lyrics, so we ran out of material and were looking round for some sort of new blood, and bumped into the Sutherland Brothers, who were a bit fed up with their band and had tons of songs, so we decided to join forces.

We did quite a lot of recording after that, because they were well-established with Island. In fact, the first thing we recorded together was 'You Got Me Anyway', which did very well in America straight out of the box, to use a horrible phrase.

There comes a point when you go, 'Hang on, we're supposed to be stars now,' and the realisation quickly dawns that it's the person that writes the song that makes the money, not the band that goes out and plugs it, unless you've got some kind of arrangement to cover that. There's only one guy in the band that's actually making any money. The rest of you are just the same as you ever were, which leads to a lot

28

of bitterness and jealousy and rivalry. So that split us up basically. That's why I left, and the band basically folded up a year later for the same reason. So I decided to freelance after that, I'd rather just put a price on me and work for whoever's prepared to pay my money and just be free to do my own thing.

JILL SINCLAIR,
MANAGING DIRECTOR ZTT RECORDS
AND SARM STUDIOS

Education: O and A levels; secretarial course – 'I think I'm still probably one of the fastest typists in the office'. First jobs: secretary – 'I think I was nineteen and I was a secretary to a financial director of a public company – I had peaked!'; Maths teacher (after teacher training college) – 'It was a very, very, very tough school. A lot of the time you were a police woman, and it was: "Where's this? Where's that? Don't behave like this! Stand up! Stop!" I can't begin to tell you some of the things that happened. But I still enjoyed it. But I also found the structure within the staff room rather stultifying, and you couldn't take a Monday off unless it was a half term, you just couldn't do it, and I found that very restricting for me as a personality.'

My brother started the first studio in the East End, and he was the reason that I got into the business, because I wanted to leave teaching and I wasn't really very sure what to do, and he said, 'Come down and see what happens,' and I took over the administrative side initially.

I didn't know what a 24-track machine was. I knew about companies administration, and I knew about the way various companies were structured from my secretarial experience, but I didn't know anything about recording studios at all. And I learned, basically. It's not terribly difficult. And I took over the running of it, I did the books, I did most of it.

NIGEL SWEENEY,
INDEPENDENT RECORD PROMOTER

Education: Royal College of Music (O levels) – 'I don't have any A levels, because at that time the pressure on the musical side of it was so heavy, I really didn't concentrate on A levels that much.' First job: music publishing junior.

Capital Radio were advertising a job for a person to work in a music publishing company – and music was the magic word – so I went along. I managed to get the job at thirty pounds a week. What I was was basically a junior, running around learning the ropes. I didn't think of it at the time as learning the ropes, but after a couple of months, I felt if I sort of concentrated and kept an open ear and open eyes, then eventually what I was doing was learning the ropes for experience, and that's what it turned out to be, and I stayed there for five years.

It was quite a happening publishing company, and I progressed through the ranks and I was then sort of the junior promotion man, and I found I was always a bit second-hand. The record companies had those records first and they were getting up to the BBC and the independent radio stations first with them, so at that point I wanted to get out.

A&R

A&R stands for artists and repertoire, and when I first got involved with Decca, Decca used to have a number of real old-fashioned A&R people, and A&R people then really were people who signed the artist, decided what repertoire the artist would record, and it was often not their own songs, and they went into the studio and they supervised the recordings with that artist.

By the time I became an A&R person, A&R people were, and indeed are, people that went out and found the artists and helped supervise their recording careers, which is what they always did, but largely were dealing with artists that wrote their own material, so really it was a question of finding the artist that had the songs that you believed in, and then hiring the right independent producer to try and help make the record.

What I realised fairly early on is that A&R by committee doesn't work, because if you play a tape to a room full of seven or eight people who are opinionated, most of them aren't going to like it or there's always a reason why they're not going to sign something. So the first thing I think is you've got to learn to have the courage of your convictions and you've got to decide, 'I love this,' and be prepared to be lonely. It's amazing how you can sometimes sign something and you play it to lots of people in the company and they all go, 'This is great,' and then you go away and you make the record and you come back with the record, and they all go, 'Ooh, I'm not so sure now.' People can shrink away from it. Then it starts to become successful and people will gravitate back towards it.

But I think a lot of it is having a belief in a particular artist, liking the way they sing or liking the songs they do, and thinking, 'I can do something with this.' And then increasingly I think A&R people have to work with the artist and have a vision of where the project fits in the market place, and A&R people are now involved in not just getting the record right, which can be that important marriage of the producer with the artist.

Having got the record right, he's then working it through the company. In the old days you'd deliver the tapes to the marketing department and that was it, you waved goodbye. Now the good A&R person is involved in the sleeve, involved in the advertising campaign, involved in thinking, 'Well, this is a particular kind of group, we want the right kind of Radio 1 session before the first single comes out, then we want to do a tour of about twelve dates, and then we want to put the first single out,' actually being involved in the whole process.

I thought, when I was offered the job, that most A&R people were dreadful. I thought they didn't really do much. But they do. It's very time consuming and erratic and hard work, but it's the best job there is.

When I was an A&R man, fifty per cent of the day was taken up with taking meetings with people who were coming in to play you tapes, and normally they were people that you knew or people that were introduced to you by somebody that you knew or someone of some kind of substance in the business, be it a journalist or a lawyer or something like that. Occasionally you'd see someone off the street, but it was very, very rare.

Somebody would always be wanting to take you to lunch, to try to sell you something, and then maybe the rest of the day would be taken up with dealing with people that were already signed, and I would say in the week probably most of the time was taken up with people that were already signed, seeing people, and then early evening you'd probably go down to the studio to see how a particular project was going, and then you might go to three gigs. And when I started, one of the best things was when you could organise it so that you could go and do four gigs in a night. People always say, 'How could he have made his mind up? He only stayed for five minutes.' But you go in and you know whether you like something or not within two minutes. There's either something about it that makes you interested or not. You get it wrong sometimes. You miss stuff. But I maintain with people, 'Never worry about what you missed, worry about what you signed, because that's what you get judged on.'

If you're going to be an A&R person, it's tough on your family. In my case I was married – and am married – and have children. I think, on the whole, if you're going to be an A&R person, it's probably better not to be married.

A&R people have got the best job in the record company. They've got the best job, but it's the most dangerous job, because if you don't actually have success, it's got the highest fatality rate in the record business. A&R people have to have hits, and if they don't have hits, they're dead. They're definitely the fighter pilots of the industry: the best job, but you get shot down.   (MAX HOLE)

INTERNATIONAL

The music business is a much harder working business than people out there like to imagine, and I'll always remember a secretary who temped for us for quite a long time and had been all the way round the company — this was when I was at Polygram — saying, 'I've worked for every single department and none of them work anywhere near as hard as international, I'm not coming back here again.'

It's a lot of meticulous work, because you have to keep every single thing absolutely clear on an awful lot of different situations, because you're talking about a record coming out in 27 or 28 countries around the world and the international job means you are like a little record company. You supply the parts. You supply the negatives to make the sleeves and the tapes to make the records or the CDs or whatever it is, you supply all the material about the artist, the biographies, the press material, the photos. You're the artery into the rest of the world.

Everything goes by you. You supply the artist to turn up to do interviews or turn up to do TV. You are in charge of knowing what they should be doing, what their plans should be, where they should be going at what time. You've got to plan it out timewise that now we go to France, now we go to Germany, now we go to Spain, now we go to America. There's no point in going there at the wrong time, because you'll completely lose the point, like there's no point in doing *Top Of The Pops* — if you could get it — when you haven't got a single out. Well, it's the same difference in France, but each country you have to know enough about it to be able to make a good decision about what should be done when.

You then need to know about the live circuit, about who are good and bad concert promoters at any given time, who are good and bad promoters for that particular group, so that you can advise the manager. If you think that the agent here in the UK, who's setting up your touring both nationally and internationally, is making a bad choice, you must tell the manager. It is up to you to tell the manager, because if you don't take that sort of responsibility, when it all falls to pieces it will all come back to you in the end, so you have to have a working knowledge of all of these things. You have to have a working knowledge of what a good marketing plan is in each of these territories, so that you can a) feel comfortable about it yourself, and b) feel comfortable about it when you're telling your own managing director and the manager of the group.

You have to be absolutely meticulous about all your details, because you're dealing with people in different countries who don't necessarily speak very good English. Everything must go into writing and everything must be absolutely clear in advance, and you must write it down and you must give it to the artist and you must give it to the other end record company and you must give it to the manager, so you're going into any given situation with the least problems that you can possibly have, because you go back and you go, 'But it said that on this piece of paper. You've had this bit of paper. You knew what it said. Now we've got to do it.' It doesn't mean to say it always gets done, but at least you're not actually disputing who did or didn't say what.

And all of these things are different in each country. They're completely different in Japan to what they are in Hong Kong, and they're different in New Zealand to what they are in Australia, so there is no one norm that you go by, so that you never stop learning things, so it's a very interesting job and I really enjoyed it. (LISA ANDERSON)

MARKETING

Marketing is somewhere beyond A&R, who sign the acts and develop the acts. You suddenly find, in most normal record companies, you're dragged into a meeting and they say, 'Hey, this is our marketing manager or marketing director' or whatever, and maybe you've been given a bit of warning of the meeting, but it could be Robert Plant or whoever, and they say, 'This is the record, you've heard the record, it's going to come out in so-and-so, there's a film around it, there's this that and the other – what are you going to do around this project? How much money are you going to spend?' The first couple of times you gulp and take a deep breath, and then steam in.

In the old days it was so much easier, because you'd just say, 'Oh, well, we'll take a half page in the *NME* and a strip ad in *Sounds*', or whatever it was. Now you've got 250 magazines out there, all clamouring for advertising space. It's a different market, and with singles sales particularly dropping, it's much harder and budgets are much tighter. I wouldn't want to be the marketing man of today.

I still keep my hand in and have plenty of suggestions, but it's developed and we've got to this ridiculous stage now where the business to be in is packaging, because you can't go into your local record shop without seeing a picture disc single, a CD single, a cassette in a special tin, that's what marketing is to some people, but the real marketers are people who can take an act and see where you're going to go. If it's a punkish type band, a rock band, a country band, or whatever, you've got to have a vision of where it's going, and hopefully get involved in the design and the whole creative element all the way through.

The great marketing people may have two hundred ideas of which only two are good, but they have ideas, and there are very few people with original ideas. You see something designed, you see even things like where to place an ad, and you think, 'Oh, brilliant,' you see something and think it's really, really good, but it's hard to keep churning it out if you're in a big record company. You've got to have a real feel for your acts.

The sad thing is nowadays we're seeing the demise of vinyl and we're losing that great thing which was the album sleeve. Designing stuff for a CD and for what will be a DAT is not quite as attractive a proposition as the old vinyl album was.   (PAUL CONROY)

Marketing obviously covers not just the selling end, but you've got to look at how the artists are going to be promoted, how they're going to be visualised, and then once that's all come together, it's actually how you're going to package them and sell them. People don't like saying it, but you can get to a stage where you look at it very much like any normal marketing operation with any item, whether it be a packet of soap, baked beans, whatever. You're dealing with a very entrepreneurial thing, but in reality the ground rules can be the same.

But at the same time one mustn't lose sight of the fact that, although it sounds a bit cold, you're selling stuff and packaging stuff, and you can have a great lot of fun along the way doing this. It can be entrepreneurial, you can use your flair, that's what you mustn't lose sight of. You've got to be good at your job, you've got to learn the way the market operates and learn all those very fundamental things that are the same, as I said, in most commodity selling, but what you've got to put on top of it is that creation and flair, which is the reason you really came into the music business in the first place.   (TONY POWELL)

PRESS OFFICE

I can only look at it from the perspective of working for Sony Music and working for what is a big record company, and when you work for a company the size of Sony Music you're not just dealing with one kind of music, one kind of person: most of the press officers here have got a roster of about forty artists, and that forty will be incredibly diverse. You might have somebody from Bros at one end to Johnny Mathis at the other. They're completely different types of people, their requirements are different, and they will take you into tackling different areas of the press.

The press office here works very much alongside the marketing department. What you're doing is co-ordinating part of a campaign with the marketing department, the radio and television department, and providing the press end to a campaign around a single or an album. It will involve everything from working on the photo session, which could well appear on the sleeve, and also the whole look of a band from the video through to the artwork, through to the photos. There has to be a common thread that will run through the image of an artist. That's where you work with other people in the company. You can't really go out on a limb and work on your own, it's very much a team with those other people.

The ultimate responsibility is making sure that you are delivering column inches that may relate to a single, an album, a tour, interviews, news items – making sure that, let's say, Bros are out there being read about, there are pictures appearing in all the magazines. Ultimately, at the end of a campaign, that's how you are judged.

At certain times it might be using skills whereby you *don't* want a particular artist or a particular news item to appear in a paper, so it's not just everything that does actually go in; you can't hold up a stack of cuttings and judge a press officer on the weight and size of the press clippings at the end of the campaign, though obviously that's important, but you need skills a lot of the time to keep stuff out of the papers, particularly now with the predominance of pop coverage in what's left of Fleet Street. That really is a very sensitive skill that a good press officer needs to have.

It's very important that you can somehow get under the skin of the artist. That obviously takes time, that you feel comfortable in setting up interviews for a particular artist, that you know they're going to get on with a certain kind of journalist. There is an element of needing to know how an artist thinks, what he or she might say, might respond in a certain situation.

One of the big differences being a press officer as opposed to a plugger is that need to be close to the artist because essentially that's what you're, if you like, 'selling'. To get a piece in *Melody Maker*, you need to know something about the artist. It's not just a question of: does the journalist like the record or not? Which is really what radio's about, because that's what keeps radio going. It's the sound of the music. What you've got to be able to do as a press officer as you approach a journalist to sell them an artist is exactly that: you are selling an artist. Yes, you will go to a journalist who you feel is going to be sympathetic to that kind of music, and that, of course, is another skill you need to have, matching an artist and his or her music with the right journalist on the right paper, but, as I say, it's very important as a press officer that you know the history of the artist that you're working with, that you know a bit about their background, what they like and what they dislike, what musicians turned them on as they grew up and so on and so forth.

I've been doing the job for fifteen years and there are growing pains, and one of the growing pains you have to go through is working on an artist whose music you absolutely love, and a number of things can happen. Maybe the press hate them, maybe the band break up, maybe the band decide you're not the right press officer for them, maybe they go and leave to join another company — all those things have happened to me, and I think you just accept it in the rough and tumble of the business.

In some bizarre way it can sometimes be easier to work on an artist whose music doesn't grab your heart and soul than it can be with an artist whose music you completely love and adore, because there's nothing that'll get in the way of the professional standards that you set yourself.

You spend an awful lot of time on the telephone. There are days when your ear aches from constantly being on the phone. But one of the nice things about the job is that you mix and meet and do business with an awful lot of different people, and to me that's always been one of the great things of working for a company that covers a wide base of music.

One absolutely crucial thing never to forget is that you are a salesman. At the end of the day that's what it takes to get your artist to appear in *Melody Maker* as opposed to somebody else's from another record company. You are a salesman. There's nothing wrong with that, but when people come into a press office, they tend to be surprised by that particular remark. (JONATHAN MORRISH)

PRODUCT MANAGEMENT

As I define it, and some other record company people would differ with it, the product manager is very much the hub of the wheel of the company.

The A&R person, who has the vision of finding the act and recording that act, then hands that vision on to the product manager, who brings it to fruition in the market place. It's his or her job to pull all the elements together, whether it be the artist, the management, and A&R person on one side, to bringing in the various departments – the press, the promotion, the selling, the designing, and marketing campaigns – it's up to the product manager to pull all those elements together, to be that hub. I have a rule that I think an artist's manager or artist should be able to call that product manager and that product manager should be able to know everything that's going on with that artist's product at any given time.

The recording budget's handled from the A&R end, because that's where the cost lies. The product manager would hold the marketing budget, which will be split into sub-sections. Some will be given to promotion, some to press and all the little sub-groups that come under marketing, and you'll then be left with a pool of money that will be straightforward, above-the-line spend: advertising and various other things that go along like that.

But the product manager becomes the key person within the operation, I think, making sure that the dream of the A&R person is then told to the public one way or another. I grew up through that area and it's stood me in good stead ever since, because from product manager, you can actually look very closely at where you want to go in your career.   (TONY POWELL)

PROMOTION

Promotion is all about getting your foot in the door and being noticed. It used to be all very giggly and you'd bring a girl along to try and get one of the radio producers out and get a record on the playlist. That's the rubbish of ten years ago. It doesn't happen any more.

And it just so happens there are a lot of girls involved now. Girls that have worked for me as secretaries, if you spot the way they're dealing with people on the telephone and they've a very good manner and they begin to know how this company works, how the acts work, how they can organise – a lot of it is organisation, getting people to the right place at the right time – and being reliable, if you see somebody that's doing that and has a good rapport with the people she's dealing with on the phone, then I tend to try and give her a chance.

You can't go to radio with every record you ever work on and say, 'This is brilliant,' because they just won't believe you. You've got to retain some credibility. And it's part of being professional, working on stuff you're not very happy with, but for the benefit of the company, you've got to try and make it happen, and realise some radio producers are crazy about records you can't understand what they're crazy about, but great, go with it. That's the professional part of it. It's no good saying, 'I like this kind of music, I'm only going to work on this kind of music,' because you'll be out of a job very, very quickly. You have to be a chameleon and be able to realise the potential of everything.

With Radio 1 there's a bit of hanging out. It used to be a lot easier when I was doing it ten years ago, when you could actually just walk into Radio 1, walk round the corridors – a very much easier relationship, not particularly professional, but you could always go in and see somebody. Nowadays you have to make an appointment or you get somebody out for lunch, if they've got an hour spare. The Radio 1 guy really has to hang out a lot during the week, try and pick his moments, try and be in the right place at the right time to see the producers. A few of them have set appointments, and a bone of contention with promotion people is that they often get cancelled, so then obviously you can't talk to the guy.

The ideal situation to play somebody a record is in their office, playing it to them, getting a response from them there and then as to what they feel. Are they going to support you? Do they think it's rubbish? Is there anything to go on? Can you persuade them any way why they should play it? If you're doing that over the phone to somebody, that loses it, you need to get to that person and have them sit down and go through the record with them.

There's a lot of artist relations involved, persuading them why they should do interviews, and a lot of the time you've got to bear in mind that whilst it's not necessarily the right thing for that major artist, they don't desperately need to be on a certain show, but if you can get one of your major artists on a certain show, then the producer of that show may look kindly upon a lesser artist on a later show. Because it's hard work to get the major stars to do the out-of-the-way things, and it's the out-of-the-way things you need for your new artists, so it's only fair you should deliver the big artists whenever you can.

It's even difficult looking after the bands and getting them there at the right time, making sure they don't go out and get drunk of a night when they've got *TV-am* the morning after, staying with them, babysitting, I've done that quite a number of times. I remember doing it with somebody who was doing *Singled Out* and they didn't want to do it, they wanted to go shopping, and I just had to be with that person all afternoon to know where they were, because otherwise they would have escaped, and that would have been a disaster. All that kind of stuff is funny in retrospect, but it's not very funny at the time.

And if you're going to be a successful TV promotion man, it means if you're successful you're going to knacker up your weekends, you're going to be working Saturday and Sunday. It's always made me giggle, particularly with EMI, there's no bonus for working Saturday or Sunday, you don't get any overtime. It seems stupid, but we do it. That's what we're about. We want to be successful.   (MALCOLM HILL)

other AREAS of the INDUSTRY

THE AGENT

A booking agent is an employment agent. His job is to find work for groups, be it at clubs, colleges or concert halls, so he'll speak to promoters, who buy the group. They agree to pay a fixed sum of money to put the group on at High Wycombe Town Hall or Brunel University or Newcastle City Hall, wherever it is. He sells the group to the club or the promoter or whatever, and whatever price he gets for the group he takes a fixed commission, which was ten per cent – now it's nearer fifteen or twenty per cent – and that's how he'd earn his money.   (PAUL KING)

THE CONCERT PROMOTER

It's very simple. In general terms he offers to pay the group a sum of money, he puts up all the money for the costs involved in staging the concert, the cost of renting the hall, the cost of printing the tickets and advertising the show, and he hopes that if he sells all the tickets, that the income is sufficient to pay all those costs and leave a profit.

You've basically got to take a view on what you think the band's worth. You've got to decide, do you think they can sell out Hammersmith Odeon? Or could they sell out Wembley Arena? Or could they sell out Wembley Stadium? It's down to you to first make that decision as to what you think they can do. You then have a conversation with the group or the group's agent. Now the group's agent may think they can sell out Wembley Arena and you may only think they can sell out Hammersmith Odeon, in which case you have an argument, and if you can't reach agreement, you obviously walk away from that there and then.

Having mutually decided where you're going to play, provided the group and the promoter and the agent, if he's involved, all agree that it's right to do a week at Hammersmith Odeon, you then cost it out and work out what the overall costs are going to be, what the residual income left is, and then agree a fee with the group. You work the whole tour on that basis. You've got to evaluate the geography of it, you've got to evaluate the venue in the area where you think it's worth putting them on, so it's quite complex. And then you've got to put your money where your mouth is, and if you're right, you make a profit, and if you're wrong, you make a loss.

The group are responsible for turning up with their equipment, which normally includes all their sound and all their lights. As a general rule the band's trucks roll up with everything they need to put on the stage to make the show possible.

The promoter's responsibility takes over from there. He has to provide the venue, the stage to put the equipment on, the seats to accommodate the audience, and all the peripheral stuff like the advertising and what have you. So it's actually quite clear. Once the trucks roll up, everything else is down to the promoter: security, the guys that unload the trucks, the guys that reload the trucks, everything. But as the shutter comes down on the hall, as the trucks drive away, that's the end of the promoter's responsibility. He is not responsible for getting the band from Birmingham to Manchester, as a general rule, or from Manchester to London or from London to Hamburg. His responsibility is confined essentially to within the four walls of the building, and if there's no stage in the building, he's got to go and get one or if there's no staff he's got to hire the staff.   (PAUL KING)

THE MANAGER

Colonel Parker, who managed Elvis Presley, summed it up beautifully one day. He said, 'I'm Elvis's manager, because Elvis says I am.' And that's all you need. You could have a four-piece band in a hut in Banff in Scotland, and if you walk in and you happen to be the local grocer and you've got a van and they need the van, you could well end up being their manager.

Now, whether or not you can stay on the roller coaster is a very different thing, but most of the skills I may or may not have I picked up as I went along. You can't go to your public library and swot up on how to be a manager. It's a gig that you learn as you go along, and you've either got the talent and the will to do it or you haven't. A lot of people come into my office saying, 'Oh, you're really experienced.'

Well, that's true, but that's not necessary. I wasn't experienced when I started with Dire Straits.

I've got a pretty good idea of the legal end of contracts, I've got a pretty good idea of how to deal with basic accountancy, but I still can't read a balance sheet. One of the great arts of management is bluffing furiously, it's making people believe you know a great deal more than you actually know and that you have far more impact on a situation. A good manager can't make a good act, but a bad manager can completely wreck a good one.

You can only work with what your act gives you. I think that's the most important thing, that if you have an act that are similarly committed in the way that you are, there is literally no limit on what you can achieve, but if you've got an act that wants to sit in a garret, scratching its bum and producing some work of high art every three or four years, and where they continue to sit in the garret and they won't do an interview and they won't go on TV or they won't play live or they won't shake hands or go to the dreaded record company dinner and get another wooden disc for their trouble, if they're not prepared to do that, then any success that they're going to have is going to be severely limited.

A lot of people say to me, and it's very flattering to hear, 'You're a great manager,' but that is because I've got an act that is exactly right for me, and vice versa. What I do is tailored to my act and the sort of act they are, and they are a mainstream, adult-orientated, straight-down-the-middle rock and roll band that's based on, I would like to think, really great songs and a particular virtuoso instrumentalist, which is Mark (Knopfler) on guitar.

What I do is a mixture of planning and execution, as far as their career is concerned, which of course I do in conjunction with them. I don't tell them what to do. We have meetings about it, we decide what we want to, what we're prepared to do, because after all they're human beings, they're not robots, I can't put them out on tour seven days a week for five years, because they'd simply fall over. So planning is a very big part of what I do and I think in career terms it's probably the single most important element, to have a clear idea of what your objectives are and how you're going to achieve them, given the vagaries of each individual's personal desires and their home situations.

There's quite a lot of administration involved, and I think if you're running a management office and your administration is not firmly in place, then any pack of cards that you're attempting to build on the top of it will quite quickly come falling down. That's the bit which is boring. And it's the same stuff that anybody who is running a small business, which is effectively what I'm doing, is faced with.

We have to do VAT returns, we have to do company tax returns, we have to do accounts, we have to do budgets, we have to do lots of logistical stuff to do with touring, making videos – relatively simple things – hiring a sound system, hiring a lighting system, getting road crew, trucks, buses, planes. Of course, I'm at the point where I can afford, thankfully, to have professional help to help me with that, so I have an in-house bookkeeper, I have a partner who's the tour manager of the group and so on and so forth, but there have been times when that hasn't happened and I had to do all that, and it was very simplistic. I had x amount coming in and y amount going out, that ought to leave z. Lots and lots of things as you go on become more sophisticated, because as you get bigger things like tax considerations creep in. If you're making a loss, that's not a consideration, if you're making a profit, it is. And if you're doing management properly, you are actually looking after the business of the group.

As a direct result of success money comes in, and, as I've said, money goes out. And if you don't keep a very tight control on that, then the whole thing will fall to bits. If you look at the history of litigation in rock and roll music, it's nearly always about money. What came in? Where did it go? Why didn't I get any?

The idea that managers like me rip acts off or dictate to them I find quite offensive, and I'm sure that my act would find it quite offensive. The idea that you are some Machiavellian Svengali type figure, that really went out towards the end of the sixties.

With the really big acts and the ones that are properly managed, their control over their own destinies, and particularly their artistic control, is almost complete. The idea that either of our record companies would put out edited singles without our approval or design covers or say, 'You're doing Top Of The Pops tonight,' is utterly ludicrous. We have never done Top Of The Pops, we will never ever do Top Of The Pops as long as I'm managing the group, and every time we put a record out Phonogram ring up and ask us to do it, and every time I turn round and tell them no. Ten or fifteen years ago people didn't have the choice. They were simply steered off towards whatever was considered right for them, which led to some rather uncomfortable situations where people who obviously didn't want to wear purple flared trousers and a bright yellow shirt with a tiger on the back were suddenly presented like that, and I think the public knows.

So, one of the things of management is to control and influence the way that your act is being presented, and not allow exploitation of them which is either economically unfair or artistically stupid or is just not right for their careers or whatever.

Another of the things of management, I think, is actually to share what you learn. When I started out, there was nobody to ask, and one of the reasons I do things like this is because I get quite a lot of people ringing me up or coming to see me or coming to seminars or whatever, who want to know about what I do, and I wish twenty years ago that I could have gone, made a few notes, learned how *not* to do it, because of course one of the things is you see people making the most ghastly, dreadful errors, but that's always with hindsight. When you're doing these things, there's no textbook to follow, you don't have a blueprint, so you have to do what's instinctively right, and I've learned that a great thing for me is following Mark Knopfler's instincts. If he feels comfortable with it, then it'll almost certainly be right for him and the band, and therefore it'll work. There's no point putting him or the group into situations with which they are uncomfortable. You have to do what's right for your act. (ED BICKNELL)

The easiest way to sum it up is a forced marriage. It involves everything from their musical career to their divorces, their moving house, whatever. If you read the contract, an artist getting divorced has got nothing to do with the manager, but in reality if the artist gets divorced, it's the manager's problem. You're dealing with their lives, because they can't function as an artist if their whole life is not together, and invariably a lot of them, especially nowadays, have a lot of success very quickly and they're very young when it happens, and they're incapable of dealing with that much success very quickly.

When you go back to the old groups, they were normally twenty-five plus when they got any level of success, but it's happening to eighteen- or nineteen-year-old kids now, who've got no experience whatsoever, and all of a sudden they have what they've always wanted, which is success, and someone puts a million quid in their hand, and they can't deal with it. And invariably, unless they've got someone guiding them, they can blow that money very, very quickly.

I think the two main jobs of a manager are one, to make sure they're as successful as they can possibly be on a worldwide basis, and secondly, once they've achieved that success, not to blow the money they've earned, because they may never be successful again, and therefore any money they earn has to be put to work for them. And I'm pleased to say that most of my acts, if they stopped tomorrow, would be okay. They'd probably have to reduce their standard of living slightly, if they had no success whatsoever from this day forward, but they've all got good property behind them and good residual income. (PAUL KING)

THE MUSICIAN

To be a working musician, you've got to be working six days a week, I reckon, and that's way above my average, which is good because I get a chance to work on my own songs at home. I don't work every week in the studios, and actually I don't think I'd enjoy it if I did, because I manage to avoid doing a lot of jingles and a lot of stuff with people I wouldn't like to work with. A lot of session musicians who work all the time, don't get a lot out of the music, and consequently don't give a lot back into it, I don't think. But they're those kind of brilliant players, who can play any kind of style, which I can't.

I'm limited in some ways, in that I know some rock 'n 'roll, I know some blues, I know some country. I know lots of bits and pieces. Some stuff I'd have to say, 'Look out!', because I'm very good at some stuff, and I get by on other stuff. People who want me, if they know where to get me, will get me. I get most of my work from people who've used me before or who know me or have seen me play or heard me play on other people's records, and they want something like that.

I didn't get a lot of pleasure out of synths, because a lot of the work seemed to me to be getting the sound, and I must admit I didn't get a lot of session work for a while there, because people wanted synths. I did actually get a couple of sessions, but they'd say, 'Oh, there's a bank of synths there. What we want to hear –' And I'd say, 'Sorry, you're asking the wrong guy.' My business card says 'Piano and Hammond Organ', so people won't make the mistake of hiring me for the wrong gig.

I think the important thing is to have a really healthy attitude and to want to do the work. I really have been very lucky that I've always worked with people I have respected, or at least liked as people. I've turned work down because I didn't like the people or didn't think their music was worth anything. I couldn't have done it. You see, I started playing from a love of the music, and that continues, and I couldn't do it if I didn't really want to play it. I'd sooner sweep streets than do that.

Occasionally, if they realise they'd be saving themselves money and you time, which is money, then they'll send you a tape, which is good because it then gives you an out, and you go, 'Sorry, I'm not available after all!' But usually you go in cold and you're on the chopping block. They'd feel there should be a piano on it, say, or an organ or something, and they think you might be the right guy for the job, and of course you then have to prove that you are, and invariably the reason that they've called you is because they know what you can do, or they think they know what you can do, and so it's usually close anyway, you're usually the right person for them. And then you hear the song and you think, 'Yeah, this is right up my street,' and you play it through a couple of times, learning the song, and then they'll say, 'No, what we meant was . . .' or 'Well, that's good, yeah, but can you bear in mind that there's this thing that the guitar plays here and could you play along with that line, but the rest of it is free . . .' or 'Keep the choruses straight . . .'. So you then work with them on it.

I don't practise. I know my C scale, but that's about it. I just play for my own enjoyment. At the moment I'm working on some songs in my studio, so I'm constantly playing, and I play all the instruments, so I'm finding new calluses and new muscles, but that's what I do, that's my recreation as much as my job.   (IAN McLAGAN)

I've never been a party-piece player at all. You get people who can sit down and whip off some fabulous kind of jazz piece or something they've worked on for months, but I've never ever done that, but what I enjoy doing, what I feel I'm good at, is just kind of blending in with what's going on and trying to find a niche within that, basically backing somebody else, so you're taking the lead from them and doing what they want. Basically you're trying to please someone by providing suitable backing for them.

I think that's a big part of playing sessions. You've got to be a bit of a chameleon. If someone wants you to be Deep Purple one minute and Richard Thompson the next, you've got to be able to do that with some sort of conviction and also enjoy doing it as well, which some people wouldn't do. A lot of people are so into their music, they're focused on one particular style. Me, I'm quite interested in doing anything. If someone comes up and goes, 'Well, I've got this sort of jazz avant-garde bit,' I'd be just as interested as if it was some kind of old folk tune or, for that matter, Adrian Belew. I get my enjoyment out of playing lots of things.

I find that the most unrewarding part of session playing is the sort of jingle thing, where you drive for an hour into town, you park the car and you rush up with your gear, and you play through this little pathetic jingle once, and it's, 'Right, fine, next, we've got the singers coming in in five minutes.' And they accept a part where you feel you could probably have played it better, and sure, they probably do as well, but it's like accept the first possible acceptable part, and get the hell out. So then you drive an hour and a half home, and you think, 'Hang on, I've been in the car driving for two and a half hours and spent half an hour carrying the gear in and played for ten minutes,' and you think, 'This is not playing.'

That's a slightly annoying bit, plus nowadays another rather frustrating element is that because of the way people work now with technology and everything, there are less and less set-ups where you turn up and there's a bass player and drummer to play with. They've usually been in and out before and they've gone, so it can be a lonely life. The lone guitarist arrives! You can go weeks on end without actually meeting another musician. So that throws the idea about getting ideas and learning off other people out of the window, which takes away a very big element of what makes it interesting. You're just working with a producer and an engineer, and possibly not even the artist – certainly with jingles and that sort of stuff you don't meet the singer.   (TIM RENWICK)

THE PUBLICIST

Your basic job as a PR is to give the most sympathetic possible response to the media for the artist, it is to see that they are represented in the most favourable light that is possible. You don't do that by ignoring phone calls. You've really got to keep in contact, that's the job, even if it's only to say, 'I'm sorry, but I cannot actually give you what you want here – I'm under instructions not to,' or whatever. At least have the courtesy to do that.

The difference between an independent PR and a record company PR is that the record company PR is basically employed by the record company and his or her responsibility is to the company, and there is a huge roster of acts that they represent, because they can't be selective in the way that I'm allowed to be selective. I can say, 'No, I don't want this account,' or whatever, so there's a slightly different relationship. So if the artist or the manager wants to complain and jump on the PR for whatever reason, he has to be very careful about doing it with the record company representative, because you can alienate the record company and also at the back of the whole relationship there is this: 'Well, you don't actually pay me, you know, the record company pays me.'

Now, if you're an independent, you're paid directly by the artist or the manager and you're directly responsible to them. If something goes wrong, it's my responsibility and it's my job, and if they get on the phone and they want to talk to me and they want to give me a going over about it, they're fully entitled to do so and I have to be in that position, but if I'm going to be in that position, I want to be in control, so if I'm not in control, I'm not going to do it.   (KEITH ALTHAM)

THE PUBLISHER

To enforce your rights as a songwriter you need to have somebody who can actually perform the copyright aspect, and that's how you would describe a publisher initially. A publisher has the right by contract to enforce all the rights of copyright, which is to grant a licence for a record, to grant a licence for public performance, to grant a synchronisation licence for a motion picture or for any form of broadcasting. That's in a sense, how the publisher-writer relationship grew up.

On top of that the publisher has further obligations, to account on time for the royalties, whatever the contract says, whether it's a 50/50 split or 90/10, and to pay punctually, and to make sure the money that writer's work is generating is collected efficiently and punctually. And thirdly it's to do the creative work.

In the early nineties, the publisher's role has actually become a bit more diverse. I actually think you're not just there to place songs. You're there to advise and, in some cases, almost manage the writer. You can get a cover recording of a song, and it can be the wrong thing. I've done that twice, where the original version, which was performed by the writer, was what we were trying to exploit. So you have an obligation to do the right thing by your writer, and if you've got a red-hot song you don't just send it out to, it doesn't matter who it is, Michael Jackson or Madonna.

My attitude is you've got to be sensible. I was accused recently by somebody of not having done very much for a composer, where I'd paid him a contractual advance, I paid him twice the contractual advance in equipment costs to get him guitars, amplifiers, home-recording equipment, we put on showcases, we've had independent press working on him, and his managers, new-found managers, said, 'What have you done for me lately?' And that unfortunately is the lot of all publishers. You're never going to be thanked by everybody because you're on a meal ticket, because if you sign someone early, you've done a good deal, you've helped them on their way, you sign a record deal and the record company suddenly takes over, and to the record company the publisher is always just a parasite.   (DENNIS COLLOPY)

Publishing has gone in two different directions. At one end of the spectrum it's quite simply a clearing house for the royalties earned by writers. For example, we have the Bee Gees. That's a good example of a catalogue of songs that needs efficiency rather than that much creativity. We will do what we can, but they are fairly self-sufficient in what they record and release and, yes, we will try and push their songs whenever possible.

Basically, at the end of the day, and we're talking about the international aspects of publishing, what major acts want is the best royalty rate available for the most efficient collection of the money, so it's a balancing act between volume and overhead. How much does it cost us to collect that money, so we can cover our heat and light, make a bit of a profit, and give them the service they need. It's a fairly straightforward operation, so you're either good at it or you need to improve on it, and if you're good at it, you'll get the business.

At the other end of the spectrum, which is more on a domestic basis and the way I'm now working, it's much more where A&R no longer is in record companies. A&R in record companies has lost its way a lot in the last few years in that they're much more an extension of their marketing departments, I would suggest. They're not finding a talent and saying, 'I don't know how we're going to develop this, but we're going to try this and this and this and maybe over a year, two years, we're going to have a bit of success,' and a lot of that's due to the fact that deal-making has become so rich, it's a huge investment on a record company's part to make an album, and also the perception in the minds of managers and lawyers has become that the record company isn't committed unless they do go in feet first at that level. It's become very difficult for A&R men to do anything other than be sure that they think they've got three hits before they even jump, and they're frequently wrong. So it's a vicious circle, but what it's enabled publishers to think of doing is crossing the divide that used to exist.

Publishers used to have songwriters who wrote songs which publishers would then present to record companies and artists and hope that record companies then recorded those songs with those artists, and then royalties flooded through to the writers. Now, more than ever, artists – bands – are self-sufficient in material, and it's become more important for publishers to help develop those bands to the point where record companies will then make that commitment, so the true A&R role of saying, 'There's something going on here – how can we try that? Meet this person, meet this mixer, meet this producer, try a couple of tracks,' is now being done by publishers more and more.

We still do get covers for writers. The west coast of America's very good for that still, and we're having success out there on that basis, but you can't rely on it in the UK, because A&R departments are not signing, as they still do in America, Whitney Houston, Mariah Carey, Belinda Carlisle. If you analyse the charts over here, which is something you always have to keep alive to, how things are changing, aside of the fact that dance records are all over the chart, aside of the dance scene, most of the UK artists who are putting records out are writing the material themselves or collaborating on the material. So you've got to plug your writers straight into the front line.   (PAUL CURRAN)

THE RECORD PRODUCER AND ENGINEER

Very generally there are two sorts of producers. There's the sort that comes up through engineering, of which I am one, and then there's the other sort that really comes from the musical side. I don't have any serious musical background, and therefore I definitely have limitations in terms of if we're going through a song or something I can't suggest that a G sharp would be a better chord than an A or something, whereas there are producers who come from more that side and sometimes there are bands who need a producer who's very musical in that sense, so I'm obviously careful to either explain to my clients or people generally know what I do now, so that sort of person doesn't come to me and if they do then I'll suggest somebody else to them.

I just figured from when I was an engineer that half the time the producer was an extra body in the control room that wasn't needed, and I would start saying things myself or the producer would say something and I would go against him sometimes, which isn't necessarily a good thing to do – well, not go against him, but suggest otherwise, and I think that's where I sort of carved out my niche in a way, because Phil (Collins) didn't need another producer as long as there was somebody who he could bounce ideas off. He had his own ideas, as he's carried on to do with every record that he's done, and we work just fine, and it's the same with me and the Police and with Sting. There's no way that they wanted a producer to tell them what to do. Sting knows what he wants to do and he just needs to relate it through somebody.

I'm not saying that I'm then not producing, because I put in my two pennyworth all the time, but they just figured there was no need to have another guy. If you've got a guy who can produce and do the engineering it's one less person to pay as well.

I think starting off as tape op in a studio is good, because you see how other people work and you get to learn how sessions work, rather than coming in all qualified up to the hilt, but you've never had any experience with working with drunken singers who don't want to sing or something. You know how to handle the whole thing better, because that's the whole thing of the arts, whether it be music, stage or the theatre, you've got colourful characters involved in it, and nobody's always just straight down the line.

I still quite often get approached by young engineers now, who say, 'How do you mike up a drum kit?' And it's incredible to me that these guys have come up, got into the position they're in, and they've never miked a drum kit, because they've come up in the eighties when most people used drum machines. And so I learned an awful lot about microphones and mike technique, you know, the best way to set up the instruments and that sort of thing.

It was hard work because coming from the engineering side you're tending to want to look at the needles and meters and knobs and things, and you suddenly go, 'Oh God, I should be listening to him singing. Was he singing out of tune? Did he have the right attitude?' Or something like that. So it was quite hard to do that to start with.   (HUGH PADGHAM)

THE RECORD PROMOTER

Whenever the window-cleaner used to come round the house, and the old gold discs are up in my study, he'd say to my wife, 'What does your husband do? Is he a pop star or something?' And Jill would say, 'No, he's a promotion man in the record business.' 'Oh, I know what that is, that's all dodgy, isn't it?'

And everyone has this idea, because I suppose in America it's very corrupt and because here years ago it was corrupt, but now it's PR – a specialised form of PR – the same as in the film world or the fashion world or ICI having someone to promote them. We promote a bunch of artists that we believe in, and all we can do is make the media aware of the people we represent, aware of their latest record, and aware of all the information that surrounds them, and convey our excitement about our artists to them. And you just hope that that's going to rub off. And hopefully we've built up such a reputation for what we do and for the enthusiasm that we have and the belief we have and the success that's come from it, that that kind of success hopefully rolls off on to the next thing that we do.

Nigel Sweeney and I get in at seven in the morning and we're here till seven or eight at night and then on the phone all night long and working weekends. It is really long hours.   (NEIL FERRIS)

We're not gimmick boys. I never have been and I know Neil never has been. And we've been together for six years now, and we're not great believers in the writing pad with the artist's name on and things like that. It's the record that's important and what's on the record. So that's what we've always based our company on, which is: what's the music like? And not how great the artist looks physically and facially and whatever. It's really just the music. So we're much keener to listen to the tape rather than meet the artist and talk about what gimmicks they're going to be doing and things like that. It's brilliant when you get a great record.

When we take on a band we take them on 100 per cent for promotion – radio and TV promotion – and I guess we tend to become more their media managers, because we're not actually interested in just the single, we're actually interested in the artist. So our main criterion is the music of that artist and once we start representing that artist, it's representing the artist right through.   (NIGEL SWEENEY)

THE ROAD MANAGER

With Rod Stewart, as crew members we had a keyboard guy and a drum guy, and the guy on stage right did the guitar and the bass, and I looked after the stage left guitars and all the acoustics, no matter who played them. I've worked for Pink Floyd and each member of the band has a man, and that's even down to there being two keyboard players up on the same riser, they still have two crew members. That's the top of the ladder, that is, man for man. That's back line, the people who're involved in the setting up of the musicians' personal gear. Then there's the PA people and lighting people.

When I was out with Def Leppard, they had twelve trucks loaded with equipment, so now you're talking twelve drivers, five coach drivers, caterers, double drivers for the long journeys, merchandising people, so it does get up to eighty or a hundred people.

The riggers go in at eight in the morning, followed by the lighting crew, the PA crew and the people who build the set. Then the back line goes in, so my day doesn't normally start till one o'clock. I go in, put our bits up, and then go about restringing guitars ready for the sound check, which is normally at four o'clock. The band come down to check the gear for half an hour, play football for an hour, and then go back to the hotel. So after sound check we just sit around till show time, which is normally nine o'clock, do the show, make sure nothing goes wrong, then pull it all down again. The bits I would pull down would take an hour, then that's me done for the day. After tearing down the show, it's all back to the hotel, get in the disco, and show your stuff!

The worst thing that can go wrong for me is a guitar lead going out. If you're up there in an arena where there's 40,000 people and a lead goes down when someone's doing an acoustic song, it's a bit lonely up there when you've got to run on and stand there and put a new lead on or try and find out what's happening to it. It's very embarrassing. Touch wood, that hasn't happened too much, but it's happened a couple of times. Maybe twice in a whole year's touring something will go down like that, but these days the gear is built around touring, and before it wasn't. It was all just built to sit in a studio.

All those days of throwing tellies and that sort of stuff are long gone, so you get guys in bands that are Buddhists and don't eat meat and don't drink on the road, but there are always two who are right ravers. They can't go out with their own band members, so they go out with the crew, so you find they're always hanging around or phoning you up. That's what most of it is – baby sitting – nowadays: 'Yeah, of course, you played well last night!'   (PAT 'BOILER' LOGUE)

THE TOUR MANAGER

Ideally, when a manager or a group decide they're going to tour, say in a year's time, the tour manager should be brought in and should work either, as I work, booking all the stuff myself, or with the manager and the agents booking the tour, making sure the tour is booked in the most efficient way, to make sure that you move round the world in the best way at the best time.

On tour, the job is the administration of the tour, which covers everything from booking the hotel, the planes, the cars and all that sort of stuff, and making sure, either through yourself or whoever you've got working with you, that the band gets up in the morning at the right time and leaves the hotel at the right time and all the bills are paid and the baggage is safely moved around with a minimum of inconvenience to the band.

There's always business to be done. You've got 'advancing' to do, which means calling up the next gigs, checking that the promoter's people have arranged for cars and baggage vans to meet the plane, checking with hotels to make sure you are preregistered as requested. There's also longer term advancing on a big tour, checking technical details, ticket sales, that sort of thing. Depending on time zones, you'd try to get as much done as you could before people are up and about.

If you're travelling, you wake everyone up and remind them what time they have to be checked out. On bigger tours, the tour manager's assistant will collect all the baggage an hour or so beforehand and go to the airport with the tickets to get the baggage and people checked in and be kerbside with the boarding passes when you arrive, so that everyone can go straight to the gate. At the other end, you go straight to the hotel and get everyone checked in, while the assistant or baggage person stays behind.

You'll most likely know what time your sound check is each day, because things normally run so smoothly you can do that. You always send the drummer down first, because drums take the most time, then you bring everyone else down and get them done as quickly as possible, so you can then get them back to the hotel, and changed and lubricated, ready for the evening's performance. With some smaller bands, for a matter of convenience and cost, they like to stay and eat at the gig and hang out in the dressing room. It depends on the band.

It's essential to try to get them on stage on time, and when they're on stage, you go to the box office and start to settle that, depending what sort of deal you're on. During the set or after the set, you get the settlement done.

If you're not in the box office, you're normally buzzing around, checking on security, making sure the lighting looks all right and the sound sounds all right. All these things come under your umbrella.

After the show, depending on the band, you either come straight off stage and into the cars and back to the hotel, or some people like to wind down in the dressing room. Then it's down to finding out what clubs there are in that particular town or, if the eating is done after the show, you have to find a restaurant, and then go to a club. Unless there's any last minute stuff that needs doing for the following day, like scrawling out memos to stick under people's doors, that's it.   (PETE BUCKLAND)

THE TOUR PRODUCTION MANAGER

When you begin a tour the production manager works right with the artist in the actual design of the show, and the production manager is hired from his experience of knowing venues around the world, where they're playing, what they want to do, what you can do and what you can't do.

With a major show for me a day starts off with rigging the show. We walk in the door, we take a look around the building, we've already done our drawings, we're aware of where everything is going to be, but then when you walk into the building after maybe four hours' sleep, you walk in, you start getting yourself acquainted with the building and what's going on, and then we jump right in and start rigging. Rigging a show takes anything between two hours and eight hours depending on the size of the show, and that's purely just hanging steels up on the beams and attaching chain motors.

From there you bring in your lighting system. A lighting system will consist of anywhere between one truck of lights and three, that are attached to these chain motors and they're assembled and then taken up into the air, which is anywhere between a two-hour job and a five-hour job, depending on the size of your tour. While that's happening your sound comes in, and the motors that weren't used to hang your lighting are used to hang your sound, so we start bringing in the sound and hanging the sound. Sound hangs fairly quickly and you usually get a sound system up in about two hours.

Then from there you build your set. Depending on the size of your set and the number of carpenters you have, it can take an hour to put risers in place or it can take four hours to build the stage. And once your set's built, the last thing you have are your monitors and band gear. Monitors and band gear take pretty much an average of between two to three hours to set up with every show – they're pretty normal every time.

You're up to four or five in the afternoon, when the band comes in and soundchecks, then you open the doors at six and do the show at eight. Once the artist goes on stage, usually I can take a breath and sit down in the production office and start making more phone calls, getting things ready for the next city.

I have a tendency to walk everywhere and look at what everybody's doing, and I tend to pace around a lot, and years ago, when I was working for Fleetwood Mac, Mick Fleetwood fixed me up with a pedometer and I think I did about six miles in one day and that was inside an arena, I never left the building.

It should be getting easier. I've been doing it for eighteen years, but

I'm still learning daily. The problem is that it's getting bigger. In the old days we used to do it and it was a piece of cake. We'd walk in – we worked our tails off, but we had a lot less people, we'd tour with a five-man crew. We wouldn't be talking about fifty people. There'd be five of us and we'd do everything – we'd drive the trucks too. But nowadays with it getting so much bigger, it's got a lot more difficult. We'd put down a piece of carpet before, a couple of risers, set up a drum kit on there and a few amplifiers and the guitar player would walk on and plug in. Now we've got computers and electronics and everything else.   (CHRIS LAMB)

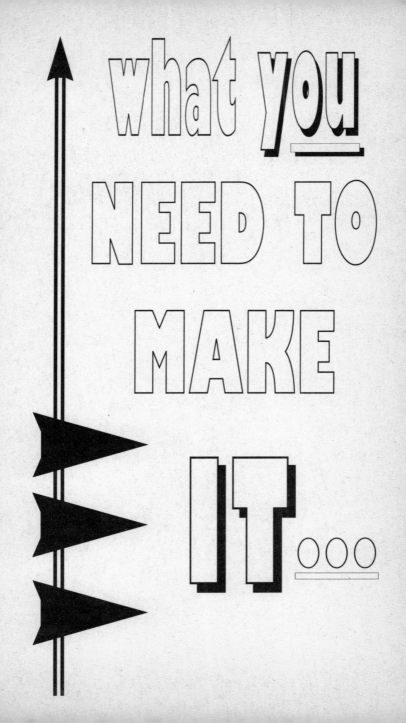

AS AN ENGINEER AND PRODUCER . . .

If·I'm giving advice to young people starting, I think if you want to do something badly enough and you're prepared basically to put your whole life into doing it, because that's what I did – I didn't have a holiday for five years at one point, I just used to work and work and work – and if you're keen enough, then I think the chances of you breaking through are very good or much much better than if you don't put 100 per cent into it, and I think you can make luck happen as well.

Obviously you have to have an ear for music just to be able to balance the music when you're mixing, and I think a small technical background is useful. I don't think you have to know how an op amp works or anything, but I think it's good to understand the physics of sound and octaves and the sonic spectrum, if it's not too corny a word.

And then I think the other very important thing, probably fifty per cent as important as all the technical side, is being able to work with people and deal with people. If you don't get on with people, then they won't ask you to work again, so I think those two sides balance each other. The diplomatic side definitely applies to a producer as well, for sure.

If you think of the other side of production being the musical side, I think probably just through experience most of them get to learn what the technical side of the studio is as well, because even if you come from that background obviously you're going to be working in liaison with an engineer, so they have to have a rapport.   (HUGH PADGHAM)

AS A MANAGER . . .

You need to be incredibly patient, you need almost to be willing to become a psychoanalyst, because you're basically dealing with people that behave like children. Success does terrible things to people, and everyone reacts differently to success, and if you look at it in terms of dealing with children, that's probably the nearest analogy I can think of, but you end up dealing with people you used to think were rational that have suddenly become incredibly irrational, and what you've got to do is not lose your temper and not tell them what you actually think sometimes in haste. If you think the guy is being incredibly irrational, they might be doing it and not realise they're doing it. You've got to actually pull them down in the nicest possible way. You've got to sit them down and make them see sense, which may take a month, it may take six months, you can't necessarily solve every problem in five minutes or that day.   (PAUL KING)

IN THE MUSIC INDUSTRY . . .

I think one of the important things to realise is that most people who get into the music business, with the exception really of what I call the professional types, lawyers and accountants, have almost certainly starved for their art at some point, and you can only do that if your love of it is so great that you're prepared to sleep on floors, eat tins of beans, munch on saveloys, until you make it, whatever that may mean to you as an individual. And I don't know of any musician, and most of the people in the management profession I know, who haven't at some time or another had to dig into those human reserves, which I can only really describe as having the will to do it.

It's something Mark Knopfler's often said in interviews. It's not just having the talent or having the back-up, having the people round you, you have to have the will to want to sleep in the back of that cold van on the way back from Bradford on a December night when there's nothing open and you can't get a hamburger and the bass player's sitting in the front seat farting and you hate his guts, all the things that happen, because the product of our endeavours is human beings – I don't manufacture pens – and all human beings have problems and frailties the same as every other human being.

If you're getting into music, you have to realise it's a highly speculative industry, it's not one in which you pass an exam. There are these courses now, but nobody's going to employ you because you've got a diploma from the Rock Biz course. It's not a profession in which very much is available to read about, you can't go into your public library and swot up on how to be a manager, it's a gig that you learn as you go along, and you've either got the talent and the will to do it or you haven't. (ED BICKNELL)

I think you have to be strong. It is without a doubt not an industry for the faint-hearted. You have to be strong. You have to believe in yourself, I think you have to believe that you're right. I think equally you have to be prepared to look at other situations. You have to look at something and say, 'Well, I know what should be done with this.' There's no point in saying, 'What do you think?' There are times when somebody has to say, 'I know what should be done with this.' I think that's important.

You have to enjoy music. However little touches you, something has to touch you, otherwise you'll never be able to tell the difference between one thing and another. I'm quite good at hits; I'm not good at the flankers, the indie hits. You definitely have to be interested in music, but I don't necessarily think that's the be all and end all.

I've never really found being a woman a problem personally. I've never noticed it being a problem, but I have been called a bitch and at times I was called the Margaret Thatcher of the music industry and the Iron Lady and all that sort of nonsense, because I think if you are strong and you are a woman, people view you more like that. And there's no doubt in my mind that if you do want to succeed in the music industry and be taken seriously as a woman, that I didn't do it the easiest way. I think it's much easier if you're strong in a quieter way, but everybody is as they are. You can't change yourself.

I don't really hold anyone in awe. I think you can respect people, I think it's important that you do respect everybody, but I don't think you need to respect somebody because God has touched their head and given them a gift. They're very fortunate they've been given the gift, but I don't think that makes them, as people, any the nicer, and often it makes them a lot less nice than people who haven't been given the gift and who maybe strive for it. I suppose that I'm lucky that I don't have that in me, though on the other hand when I was young and in the business I was terribly brash and have got still a very strong reputation for being very brash and very outspoken, but partly, I think, because I don't think, 'Oh, it's so-and-so, I shouldn't say that.'

I've learned. I think I'm much more moderate now. I've learned the fragility of the artist's ego and the things one hasn't to say, rather than what one has to say, so I've learned that very much the hard way, and I've also learned the real truth in that old truism: 'Least said soonest mended.' I have learned a lot to keep my mouth shut.

One thing I have found is that the more innately talented the person is, often the easier they are, the less ego they have, the more willing they are to listen to other people, the less problems, the less insecurities they have — Phil Collins is a typical example — people that are genuinely talented and who work very hard for it, and don't get totally into the star trip and are aware of the fragility of the nature of the whole business that we work in and also in some respects, dare I say, the inconsequentiality of what we do.

Some A&R people I have met, I wouldn't give the job of looking after my dog to, but maybe they have been lucky, and a lot of this is luck, there's no doubt that there's a large element of luck. Having said that, I think people can be lucky once, maybe twice. I think people who have consistent track records are because they are good, they work hard, and they have luck. You definitely need all of those.   (JILL SINCLAIR)

AS A PRESS OFFICER . . .

Ability to get on with people I think is absolutely crucial; the love of music, because you still need that; the love of the printed word. I don't think you can be a press officer without any of those requisites. From there on in I think it is just a question of being professional.

I think the public tends to look at the record industry as being a very glamorous job, and it is, and I hope I never lose the excitement that glamour gives me, but you can't work in it and survive on glamour. There's an awful lot of hard work and graft and science to what you have to do. You can't just exist being fuelled by the showbiz aspect of it, because you just won't last five seconds.

To enjoy it to its full, it's absolutely crucial never ever to lose sight of what brought you into it in the first place and that sense of excitement you felt when you were still buying records. I think that's absolutely crucial that you wander into record shops and buy records, that you try and remember what it was like when you were fifteen, that's absolutely crucial, because otherwise you do lose touch with the people that are buying records and paying your salary.   (JONATHAN MORRISH)

AS A PUBLICIST . . .

I think being articulate is pretty important for anybody when they're in a business which is to do with communication. If you can't articulate your campaign or your attitude to the artist or the person who's going to employ you, it's pretty difficult to convince them that they should take you on in the first place, and also, of course, it's important in relating a story. If you've got to get on the phone and tell some poor battered journalist, who's had three PRs on the phone to him already that day, that he should write a story on this particular subject, you'd better be pretty persuasive and have a good idea of what that journalist might need, because he or she has got a lot of other things to do during the course of the day, and if you haven't got a good argument and a good story, then the next time you ring up they're going to be 'in a meeting' or 'on the other phone' or they're 'going to ring you back'. So from that point of view of course being articulate is important.

I really think that probably the journalistic thing does help, if you've got some basic journalistic background, because a) it makes you realise the problems that the journalists have got, when you're dealing with them, and you don't get too jaundiced about the fact that they can't do certain things or you get let down with this, that or the other, because you know the structure is not always in the hands of the journalist doing the interview and that the editor, the sub-editor, the layout man and everybody else have a say in what eventually happens to the finished piece, so you have to have a certain sympathy for the guy who's having to do the writing, and that gives you an understanding of how that works and you then don't make the mistake of going off the deep end with a writer because when the piece comes out it's got a jaundiced headline and a rotten photograph and been chopped to pieces, because he doesn't control that situation. So, that sort of thing and the fact that you do occasionally need to write, if it's only putting together a new release and the writing of biographies, which is very useful in PR, so that background is very handy and gives you a good starting basis.   (KEITH ALTHAM)

AS A PUBLISHER . . .

I think you have to be musical. That sounds like an obvious requirement, but it's not always the case in other areas of the business. I think you have to have an understanding of songs, an understanding of how songs are written. The role of a publisher, I always feel, and I do say this to people, is to help the writer become as good as he can be. It's like being a trainer. The talent may be there, but you've actually got to keep them stretched and fit and not complacent and to try new things. You've got to keep it fresh and moving forward.

If I have a musical understanding and appreciation, I can relate to my writers, mixers, producers, artists, in that way, and hopefully they will speak the same language. So if I'm advising them to work with certain people, I'll be able to rationalise why that is and why it will be worth trying. Not everything works, but if you try and it does work, that's fine, and if it doesn't, move on to the next. On a creative level I think that's the most important thing. It's a very broad answer.

On an administrative level, a managerial level, I've got copyright, royalties, finance, legal and creative, as well as general office staffing considerations, so you have to be a jack of all trades, and I suppose within record companies the MD of a record company has all the same elements, but maybe stepping back. Each department within a record company has a very specific role to play within the overall group. What publishing is, is a smaller, leaner machine, because the return is smaller, it's a nickels and dimes game, and we do basically wear more hats, which ultimately, I find, makes the job more interesting. I think it's more interesting to have the full spectrum to be responsible for.   (PAUL CURRAN)

IN A RECORD COMPANY . . .

Spunk, I suppose. A sort of streetwise attitude. There are people in this company who think if a kid's been to public school, he ain't been to the university of life – that sort of thing – but there are plenty of kids who go to whatever school, who've got bottle, who can stand in a room and talk to someone, hold conversations. It's confidence, it's the old Colgate ring of confidence you've got to have. O levels and A levels and university degrees – obviously it's important. Education makes you be able to stand up on your own, but there are plenty of people who had great educations who couldn't go to dinner with George Harrison and talk to him on a level.

It depends on the role. If you're going to go into the financial side or a lawyer or business affairs, obviously education is the all-important thing. If you're going to go into the art department, you've got to be good at art. If you're going to be a plugger or a salesman, then you've got to have almost the old foot in the door, so you can go up to Radio 1 and be very pleasant to them. You've got to have a look as well. I think the great people I've known in the business have got that feel. They've got a flair for fashion. Even if it's Maurice Oberstein (Polygram chairman) in a silly hat. At least you feel there's someone there who's a character, and the people I've got the greatest respect for in the music business are people who've got something about them, and it's a bit of a dying breed.

Also, good health; being able to take knock-backs. You've got to give up a lot of social life and be prepared to go through at least one divorce anyway, like me. You've got to have the ability to get on with other people, be prepared to suffer agent's tummy and this, that and the other.

There's lots of things you have to put up with, but if you still get a thrill at the end of the day, it's more than most people do in their jobs. I don't understand how most people get up and do a 9—5 job. I don't know what I'd do now with the time, if I had that amount of time on my hands. I want to get in here in the morning.

I'm usually in here about a quarter to eight, eight o'clock, and very rarely get out of here much before 7.30 or eight o'clock, and that's usually to go to a gig or whatever. The luxury I give myself is a season ticket at Chelsea to go and scream my head off, and that is really my relaxation at the end of the week, and if you follow them for a number of years you know that gives you even more ulcers, but I think you've got to lead by example and I'm very much a team player. I believe in total commitment and total effort, and I think anybody who knows me will say we all have a good time, we all muck in.

The music business – it's your whole life really. I've long since lost all my friends who weren't interested in talking about the music business. It's like religion. You do get very wrapped up in it. When I came in the business, I was killing to come in. There still are kids who come in that way, but to get them to put in quite the same amount of time and effort and have the feel, it's very difficult. Maybe it's just because they're younger and they want to go off to an acid house party or want to run off to something else.

I was interviewing people for a job in the promotion department. Well, I wanted someone to come in and be like a young Judd Lander

(Chrysalis Promotions Director), someone who would play bagpipes naked through St Anne's Court for a bet, who'd go up to Radio 1 dressed as a giraffe. That's where the fun element of the business still is, but you worry that there aren't kids out there with the bottle to do it any more.   (PAUL CONROY)

You need different qualities for different things. If I'm going to hire a promotion person, I want someone who I feel could change my mind about a record, someone who's got a bit of front, a bit of bunny, a bit of lip, who might make you laugh. If you go to a radio producer and they don't like your record, it doesn't matter if you're the greatest promotion person in the world, they're probably not going to change their mind until the record's so high in the charts they can't not play it, and equally they might love it. But sometimes, in the middle, a record might need a couple or three plays before people get it, and a great promotion person is someone that can persuade them. So you want someone you feel could change a no into a yes.

In A&R, you need to be lucky. And I think you've got to be very committed. I think it's impossible being an A&R person unless you really are a fan, I think you've really got to love it. You've got to be quite opinionated. Arguably one of the most successful A&R people is (Sire's) Seymour Stein, and one of the things I've always realised about Seymour is he's got good instincts, he's very passionate about music, very knowledgeable about music, and has made a lot of very good signings, but he's very astute at business.

So I think you need to be lucky, I think you need to have great instincts, be passionate about music, but be quite good about money. And then you've also got to be good at dealing with artists, because artists are sometimes erratic, and often the better the artist, the more erratic.

You also want someone you feel is really going to win, because also A&R is sometimes partly getting there earlier than other people, so in A&R you want someone quite competitive, someone who hates losing even a stupid little game of noughts and crosses.

In marketing you need to be very, very organised, very together. You need to understand the economics of how much do you spend to get this amount of sales, but again you need to have a bit of flair and you need to have some instinct and you need to have some feel for the music.

The best people in record companies are people that have a passion for music, because often I've met people who've come into marketing from advertising or from other areas and often they find it difficult, because there is a big difference in marketing a Sisters Of Mercy record and marketing a Nick Kamen record. You've got to be able to feel and understand the difference in the music to be a good marketing person. So I think you've got to be passionate about the music.

I still think that. I think the record companies that are the best run are staffed with a lot of people that are fans and have a kind of feel for the music. You've still got to have some lawyers and accountants, and I've got nothing against lawyers and accountants, and some lawyers and accountants are very passionate about music, but I remember the guy that we hired as the marketing manager, who in the interview was probably a little nervous, and I thought was a bit quiet for us – it turned out he's not quiet at all, but he was nervous – but the thing that sold him to me was he said to me, 'I went to Liverpool Polytechnic because I loved the Beatles so much and I wanted to go to Liverpool,' and I thought, 'I'm sold.'

Press and promotion need a lot of front, marketing's a combination of being together and flair, and A&R have to be mad!   (MAX HOLE)

I think that being tenacious is the most important thing probably, hanging on and keeping at it. I think it's a good idea, which is not at all fashionable now, not to want to do it too fast. When you're a secretary, there's no point in wanting to be the managing director the day after tomorrow, you do have to go through a couple of other phases, and I've seen people fall at fences because of that, people who had great promise, just wanting to go too fast. I've also done that to people. I've said, 'Okay, I'm going to give you a big promotion.' I've given them big promotion and they have crumbled under it, because it is much tougher than people imagine. I think that you must take it stage by stage, and the best training for it is knowing each bit as you go along, not so you can fall back on it, so that you can go backwards, but you really know an area, then you're mature enough to go into the next one and you're completely sure about what you're doing.

That is advice for somebody who has got no particular qualifications. I didn't have any, and I started off as a secretary, and now I'm a managing director – this is extraordinary! I don't know how I've done it myself, but I've just been tenacious, and I've done it, I think, honestly. I've done it without lying and whatever I've said I'm going to do, I've genuinely tried to do it and not just pretended to try to do it, and so people trust me. I think people trusting me is probably the key to having got where I am today.   (LISA ANDERSON)

You have to have a pretty thick skin for some of the rantings and ravings that one has to go through in dealing with artists that have just maybe heard their record's gone down the chart and they believe it was going up. Where are they going to come looking? They're going to come looking for you, and you just have to sit and explain to them.

I put great store on making sure that you do form a good strong bond with your artists and work with them and never really try and pull the wool over their eyes – if there's nasty things to be said, make sure you say those nasty things to them, but try and lay the groundwork before you do. Don't be a bull in a china shop. (TONY POWELL)

AS A RECORD PROMOTER ...

Honesty is important, because too much goes under the bridge. If you're a dishonest person and keep being dishonest when you're talking to radio producers and deejays and TV producers, it'll come back on you eventually and you just won't get anywhere. (NIGEL SWEENEY)

AS A ROAD MANAGER ...

I think ninety-eight per cent of it would just be getting on with people. You could be the brainiest person in the world on the electricial side and the best guitar player in the world on the roadying side, but if you don't get on with people you just wouldn't last. You've got to have some sort of character that they all like, because you're dealing with musicians, and there's a big ego thing there for anyone to get up on stage and sing – you've got to be way out there anyway – so you've just got to deal with it. In a band you've got five people who are all different, and you've got to get on with all of them. That's more than half of it, just getting on with them, and knowing how to talk to them, because musicians would have you running round getting them cups of tea and doing all this for them, if you let them get away with it, and there's ways of telling them to get lost without telling them to get lost. That's why they get us old boys in, because we won't take any nonsense off any twenty-one-year-old millionaire. We won't have it. (PAT 'BOILER' LOGUE)

AS A SESSION MUSICIAN . . .

You have to be fairly philosophical, otherwise – you do meet people who get so embittered by situations they find themselves in that they jack it in and say, 'Forget it, I'm going to be a plumber.' Most musicians have periods where they question what they're doing and wonder whether they might be happier driving a mini-cab without all this stuff to worry about, because of all the business of changing fortunes. The best musician in the world, one year you can go out and earn a hundred grand or something, have a fantastic year, then the next year, by no fault of your own, the phone may not ring. You miss a few breaks and you could struggle by and earn ten grand, and it wouldn't be any reflection on your playing or performance or behaviour or anything. It's just one of those things.

So you can have this horrible situation where you're doing very well one year, and a year later you're then required to pay tax on those wonderful earnings, and of course in that interim period you haven't earned very much money, so you find yourself with a whacking great tax bill that you can't actually meet, and you struggle for about three years to pay it back, and that happens to a lot of people.

It's all very well the accountant saying, 'Put it away', but it's not as easy as that, as we all know, and the temptation is obviously if you're doing very well one year you kind of assume that this could well go on. And in fact the business people, the accountants and lawyers, assume that as well. As far as they're concerned, if you're earning this much this year and you've earned that much the previous year, you're going to earn this much the following year, but of course it doesn't follow in music. It's like any freelance thing. You have no guarantee at all you're going to get more work.   (TIM RENWICK)

AS A TOUR MANAGER . . .

A reasonable understanding of business, definitely an overall technical knowledge, so that you can talk about sound systems and lighting systems and sound and lighting boards. You need to know a bit about set design and set operation, and a bit about electricity, because to control a tour you have to have a bit of knowledge about everything really. You have to have an understanding of truck loading and the average speed of trucks across the ground. You've got to have quite a broad knowledge of things really. There's no training for it. It's the sort of thing you have to learn as you go along. In my case, I was lucky, because I knew quite a bit before I got involved with the Faces, and then the Faces being quite a small band in England and escalating so rapidly in America, it was all learned very, very quickly, at the best time, at the best level. (PETE BUCKLAND)

AS A TOUR PRODUCTION MANAGER . . .

Let's say you wanted to become a production manager, you just don't walk in and say, 'Hey, I'm a production manager.' You have to know the venues that you're playing. Each venue has a different capacity, a different shape to it, and you can do certain things in some buildings and some things you can't do, and it's just knowing what you can get away with. You've just got to get out there and do it. You can't just learn it overnight.

You've got to know what everybody's doing. You've got to understand the rigging of a show, what it takes to hang a show in a building. You've got to understand weights – how much weight loading you can put on steel – just a basic understanding of that. You don't have to be an engineer, but you have to have a good idea of what's going on. You've got to understand logistics, as far as the location of cities is concerned, what it's going to take to get from city to city, if there's mountains in the way, if you've got to take a ferry, which happens a lot in Europe, all these things have to be scheduled in and judged like: can we get there? And we have to get from city to city in a certain amount of time and it takes a certain amount of time to build the show, so you have to be aware of your mileages.

You've got to know a bit about lighting, because every lighting designer in the world would love to have as many lights as he can have. Your job is to keep the price reasonable, so you have to sit and say, 'Well, why do you really need this?' And you have to know what you're talking about. Same goes with sound. You have to have a little knowledge of sound, because sound engineers will want the moon and they'll keep asking for it, and somebody has to be there to maintain a semblance of order and budget. (CHRIS LAMB)

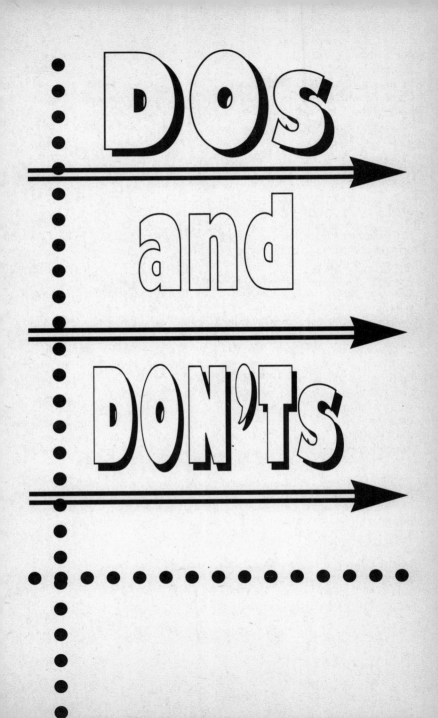

DOS and DON'TS

IN MANAGEMENT . . .

Two golden rules. Don't handle your artists' money. They can always turn round and say, 'You're useless,' but they can't say that I stole off them, which I've no interest in doing anyway. We do handle some of their money, just because it's logistically easier to do it, but royalty income goes to their accountants and we get our commission from the accountants, and that's fine.

The other golden rule is: don't get too involved in what I call 'personals'. I have actually had a major act, who I represented, ring me up at home at two in the morning to tell me his budgerigar died. I have no interest in being a nanny to grown men or women who happen to be in music for their living, dealing with their mortgages, dealing with the bicycle tyre that burst, faffing around with cars, girlfriends, wives, tickets. I won't, for instance, get them tickets for shows. If they want to go and see Joe Bloggs, let them go down to Shaftesbury Avenue or ring a ticket agency or go to the box office. I will not under any circumstances be a ticket agent, and they know that.

My act don't ring me at home very often, hardly ever. We don't have a relationship where I talk to them every day to take them daintily through the flowers of their career. I've got my job to do, they've got their gig to do.

This business of girls coming on tour. As we've said many times, if you were working in a bank, your wife wouldn't come and sit in the lobby of the bank and look at you working behind the counter, so why do they come to Spain? Because it's glamorous. Now, of course, we're at a point where it's not particularly glamorous and most of the girls have long since realised this.

But those sorts of things come into it, and management is very much keeping human relationships all up in the air, and trying to work out those things without getting bogged down in them. Generally speaking, I won't get involved in personal stuff, and it was a major reason why one artist I looked after and I fell out, because he expected that as part of the service and I wasn't prepared to give it, and in a way it became a battle of wills as to who was going to give in, and we eventually decided to split, because I couldn't get excited about his budgie – or its demise. And I certainly wasn't interested in things like employing nannies.

Another thing which comes up a lot in our profession, I didn't get into music to have a sound system or a lighting rig or a trucking company. I got into music because I like music, and I still like music, but I didn't get into it to have several tons of light bulbs and steel and wooden boxes in the back of a pantechnicon going to the NEC. It's boring. I know a lot of people in our business who've got into that. They invariably have got out of it again – and some quite disastrously.

The idea of having lots of spin-off businesses is to me of no interest. There are some people in my profession who are empire builders. They want to have lots of bands, they want to have publishing companies, record labels – I mean, I've been offered record labels like they're going out of fashion. You know, 'Pick your own colour!' For what? To have more paper going across my desk?

I think that the best management situation is between a manager and possibly not more than two acts. We've got two here, of which my partner looks after Paul Brady, so apart from his deals I don't really get involved, and if you look at most of the successful management relationships, they're one on one: Bruce Springsteen and John Landau, Elvis and the Colonel, John Reid and Elton, dare I say it, the Straits and myself, Peter Grant and Led Zeppelin. He had Bad Company, I had Bryan Ferry for a while and Gerry Rafferty many years ago. Generally speaking, everybody dabbles, and you soon find out that what you're really comfortable with is the thing that you're most in love with. And I once summed it up to somebody. They said, 'Why don't you have more acts?' I said, 'Well, put it this way – Dire Straits are a vocation and the others are a job.'   (ED BICKNELL)

IN THE MUSIC INDUSTRY . . .

One of the things that's a fallacy in this industry – or one of the things that's true, but is wrong – is that ninety per cent of the people in this industry look on it as a bit of a laugh and good fun and they stroll in at ten thirty in the morning and stroll out to lunch at one o'clock and stroll back at three and go home at five. A lot of people do that and have a great time for a short period of time.

If people are thinking of going into the record industry and are looking at that side of it, and thinking, 'Isn't it great?' And go to a few gigs, have a company car, a few ligs, get drunk, that's not the industry, that's not what it's about. Underneath, get past all of that, there's a real industry there and real business to be done, and it's about believing in things you do, and going for it. You've got to work very, very hard, and if you're prepared to work incredibly hard, then it's a really rewarding industry.

Most of the people in this industry, I think, are frauds, but there are a handful of people who aren't, and those are the people who are moulding the industry and are doing really well. They're the people who will continue to do really well. They're the people that are innovative, they're the ones that are honest, and they go for it. Then there's this periphery which is an awful lot of people, who basically tell terrible fibs, haven't got a clue what they're doing, and are wasting everyone's time. And that, unfortunately, is a huge proportion of the industry.

If you believe in yourself and you really believe you want to get into the record business and do something, you can do it. Anything's possible in this industry, which is the great thing about it. (NEIL FERRIS)

IN A PRESS OFFICE . . .

I think probably two of the best pieces of advice that were ever given to me are two of the simplest: one, always return your phone calls, and, two, when you tell somebody you'll send them a record, then do it. That way you build up a sense of trust and understanding with all the journalists that you have to deal with, because that's really what journalists want to know: when they phone up a record company press office, they want to speak to someone that they know, so that they know where they stand.

You've got to remember that you really are providing a service for them, and there is nothing worse for a journalist who's on a deadline and who needs something quickly or needs a quote, that they then don't get it, because it makes their life impossible for that particular moment and when you're trying to pitch, say, a brand new band to that same journalist in three months' time, they're going to think, 'Hold on, this guy just didn't deliver the last time I spoke to him,' so it's very important that you are – I can't think of a better way of describing it – professional – that you carry out what you say to somebody you're going to do. (JONATHAN MORRISH)

IN PUBLIC RELATIONS . . .

Whatever the situation you should not simply leave a journalist hanging. If you know that a difficult or delicate situation has developed involving an artist, your immediate reaction is, 'Oh God, no, I don't want to have to talk about this,' but you mustn't do that. If you do that, you create another kind of problem, which is simply by being unavailable, they are then going to take the next course of action, which is either to try and get direct to the artist or find somebody who's perhaps got a less qualified version of what has happened or is likely to put it in a slightly less pleasant light than you might do yourself.

My advice is, don't get pushed into too extreme a position, even when you're dealing with sensationalist newspapers, because if you erect a wall between yourself and the media, someone will write on the wall and it's usually not very pleasant the kind of things they write on walls. Really the job of a PR is creating a bridge between the artist and the media. Sometimes you have to shut the bridge occasionally for a bit or let only one bus over at a time, but it's a great mistake actually just to brick the thing up and try and stop people coming through, because they'll either swim round it or under it or write on the wall or find some way of doing something that can be a great deal less controlled than what you feel you're effectively doing by just trying to put an umbrella over the whole thing.

And sometimes also by doing that you will draw more attention to the artist than you would do if you were a little more open-handed about things. Journalists will then say, 'What is this protective screen? What's it all about? He must have something to hide. And if he's got something to hide, it must be worth writing about, so we'd better find out about this.' There's more of an incentive to dig it out than there would be if you were more open about things.

Another criterion I've tried to keep to has been not to represent obnoxious people and not work with obnoxious people in terms of management. Sometimes it does happen by accident, particularly if it's new people you haven't represented before, but you can very swiftly change that. And the reason for that is two-fold: a) it's obviously a selfish thing — you don't want any more aggravation than you've actually already got, and this is a very stressful line of business to be in and there's lots of anxiety and sleepless nights sometimes, so you don't want to take on more trouble than you've already got, and b) if you're actually going to represent somebody who, however talented, turns out to be a complete and utter prat, you don't really want to have to take that person to meet contacts that you've built up over the years and are useful to you and helpful and co-operative, and then find that they're alienated by this creature that you've brought in to meet them, because you want to go back to that person with somebody else later on. I've been lucky by and large, but there are a few I've put on the hit list who I'd never represent again.   (KEITH ALTHAM)

IN A RECORD COMPANY . . .

You have to be careful that you don't promise the earth, which is what a lot of people do and I'm glad to say I avoided doing, that a record will be a hit if . . . Wrong move, don't do that, because if it isn't a hit, you've cried wolf by this time and they won't believe you next time. It's very important to keep your credibility with the artists and the managers, so that you're not promising things you can't come up with, and that's something that's very prevalent in the music industry, as it is in many companies, it's not endemic just to us, but it's something I've found has stood me in very good stead and I think it's something everybody should try to do, which is not to lie, because if you lie, you get caught out one too many times, you're not credible, and if you're not credible you won't get a better job. Of course, there are exceptions to that rule, but I'm not it, I didn't get this way by lying.   (LISA ANDERSON)

If you're always around artists, which you most probably are likely to be in the job that you do, especially in the marketing area because artists will want to tell you how they perceive themselves, I think you have to have an honest and open relationship with those artists. Where possible, you must keep them always informed of the good news and the bad news. If the record's not selling, you've got to tell them that, you've got to try and explain some of the reasons why it's not. You've got to be as honest as possible with the people around you and form good solid relationships with the people as you go along. That has always been the base I worked off. It's a hard pill for artists and managers to swallow sometimes that they might find their career on the wane. What you might have to do is soften the blow, but, as long as you've been honest with them all the way down the line, somewhere along the line it will pay dividends, I think.

One bit of advice I'd give people is where possible try and get to be better at what you do by learning more, and don't be afraid to ask and find things that will make you better, like I found courses.

There's a great amount of information out there that you can find and you can go and do it, like I did at one stage, because I felt that I was lacking in a couple of areas; I had private tutorials, because I felt that I needed to learn and I needed to learn on a one-to-one basis – I didn't want to sit in a room and show people I didn't know anything about this – so I arranged some private tutorials, which was great.

I see my job, and have always seen my job, as much as educating myself in what I do and getting better at what I do, I also see it as a job of educating artists and managers, making them understand a bit more of how our business works.   (TONY POWELL)

ON THE ROAD . . .

Don't let yourself be walked over, because then you'll find that if they do take you on the road as a friend, you know the old saying, business and pleasure don't mix, because once they start getting a few quid, you'll be running around twenty-four hours for someone who used to be your best mate, but who now is a big pop star.   (PAT 'BOILER' LOGUE)

AS A SESSION MUSICIAN . . .

Basically, have a good attitude. Go in wanting to do your best, not thinking, 'Oh, it's going to be easy,' because it never is then. Go in looking for a bit of a challenge and hoping to learn something, because you always do. If I've got a piano solo or a piano part on one of my own songs to work on, I'm no good as a task-master for myself, I just won't be bothered. I'll play it through once and I'll think, 'Oh, that'll do, it's only me,' but I couldn't do that for other people. They'd expect something from me and I'd give it to them.

And do be on time. In fact, be early. I always make sure I'm early, definitely, because I've worked with people who like to dock you two or three minutes.

I always take a couple of bottles of water with me. I like a drink, but I don't like to drink while I'm working – it's nice to keep focused. But I constantly need liquid refreshment. And I've also stopped drinking coffee, for my own peace of mind, and I don't need that jumpy feeling when I'm working. I like to be nice and calm and busy. (IAN McLAGAN)

Play. At any excuse, play anything and everything, everywhere. Don't ever turn anything down. The most dodgy sounding session, whatever the project happens to be, you're going to turn up and you're going to meet a producer, you're going to meet the studio staff, the engineer, you're going to meet other musicians. You make friendships. It's useful for you. You learn things from other musicians. The actual piece of music you're playing might be a load of old rubbish, but you make contacts and you learn things. I've heard people say, 'I got offered this, but, no, I wasn't interested,' and you see them three months later and they go, 'I haven't got any work.' And you think, 'Well, you should have taken that session, and maybe that would have led to . . .'. That's what it's about: one thing leading to another. So you really can't afford to be too picky really, you just have to get in there and make the best of what's available and hope it leads on to different things.

An ironic thing about the whole freelance music business is a lot of it's down to turning up on time. That's the key thing that'll lose you work – if you're late or unreliable or erratic or turn up drunk or whatever. A lot of it is actually being there half an hour before you're supposed to be. It sounds pathetic, but it really is quite an important part of it. You can be a brilliant player, but if they're not sure you're going to show up, then you won't get hired, however good you are. You hear of these odd brilliant players who like a drink, and it's like: book him early in the morning. If you book him after two o'clock, forget it. If the pubs have been open a few hours, the guy's going to be lego. So you book him early in the morning.

But you've got to be a good player to survive that. There's one or two people I know who are fairly unreliable, but will turn up at ten o'clock and they'll be straight and they'll play fantastically and then go off and get drunk down the pub. But basically you have to be very reliable, as conscientious as you can be.

Of course, everyone gets these odd horrible nightmare things where you turn up half an hour late and there are sixty people looking at you, which is just awful, it's the worst thing. And then you have to sit down and try and relax and play properly after dashing through the West End, covered in equipment, panting into a studio half an hour late, it's just awful. So, anyone thinking about being a session player has got to consider that. That's the bottom line. You *have* to be there, wherever you're required to be, in a suitable condition to play.

If you're into doing sessions and you enjoy doing them, you can't stop, you can't take a week off. I've made a few mistakes like that. One particular company that I was doing a lot of jingles for – I was getting quite a lot of work at the time and I rang them up and said,

'I'm not really interested in doing these jingle sessions any more.' 'Thank you, okay, fine.' And you never hear from them ever again. And I soon learned that that's not the wise thing. You have to accept everything. There's this very cut-throat situation. You are struck off the list and, of course, there's eighteen other guys that are all: 'Yes, I'd love to do a jingle. Eight in the morning? Yes, I'll be there.'

You have to have an open mind, and a bit of enthusiasm as well. There's nothing worse than being an artist in a studio and looking round and there's a bunch of guys picking their noses. You're required to give something. I enjoy it, so hopefully I give out as much as I can to try and encourage other people.   (TIM RENWICK)

AS A SONG WRITER . . .

To put even two to three songs on a cassette is a bit dangerous, because unless the first one has some sort of impact, they're not even going to go on to the second one. I've been in cars with A&R men where they take a tape from the floor of the car, stick it in, give it ten seconds, if they don't like it they fling it out the window. I've seen them do it. I've seen managers do that. I wish I could be more positive about it. Obviously the stronger the song the better the chance, and as a result of that the stronger the demo. If it sounds attractive or exciting as a demo, then there's a better chance of them listening on to the chorus.

I wouldn't take the chance on sending them a skeleton of an idea. It has to be pretty well presented as a finished record, in as much as the whole arrangement idea is there, all the important parts to the structure of the arrangement are outlined. Maybe you don't have to say exactly what sounds are used, but you have to outline the rhythm of it and the arrangement, and that takes time.

When Terry Britten and I do a demo, sometimes you can write the song in half an hour, but the demo will take us between a week and two weeks on average, and that's working every day on it, five days a week. That's with 24-track equipment, sequencers, mastering on to DAT, best possible quality, and I know what it's like in America – we had a No 1 and everybody's on the phone for a month. After that month the phone stops ringing and it's back to the drawing board. And unless you come up with another red-hot song, you're just like the next guy. There's no 'Well, this is it, we're now established.' You've still got to deliver, one after the other, and I think that's how it should be too.

I haven't really been aware of how the business side of it works up until the last four or five years. I've forced myself to get into it, but it has been a case of forcing myself to understand the contract, clause by clause, and where the money comes from, how you get it in. It's certainly worth doing.

I think it's your responsibility to yourself to understand what you're signing. There's no other way round it. If you have a lawyer look at a contract for you, which you have to have – great – you must do that or legally it isn't even binding, but even if a lawyer says to you it's fine, I think it's just letting yourself down unless you read through the contract. If you don't understand it, because the wording is very obscure at first – you *do* get used to it – go back to the lawyer and say, 'What does this mean? Tell me in plain English what this means.'

And as long as you can say to yourself, 'I understand what I'm signing,' then I think there's a lot of bitterness you can avoid, because sooner or later, if you sign something which is a bad deal, it creates bitterness between you and maybe your manager or you and the lawyer or you and the publishers or the record company, and then it affects you and it stops you writing, and I've seen that happen to writers. It's poison in a way, because it's negative and it can breed a certain bitterness which, I think, comes out in the writing. I can actually see it in writers, who have suffered under that, and it doesn't do any good. They have to pour it out, and where do they pour it? They pour it out in their writing, and who wants to hear about it on the radio?

You've got to protect your copyright, that's the main thing. You wrote the song, it's your creation, and the copyright should belong to you. Don't let anybody tell you any different, and especially these days, because media is getting more and more, and copyrights are becoming more valuable. We wrote 'When I'm Dead And Gone' twenty years ago – we still hear it on the radio, it still makes a lot of money. It's amazing. It's not just a case of having a hit and there's a peak earning period – well, there is obviously – and then it disappears. It doesn't disappear. Every hit I've ever had since 1970, before that, has maintained a certain income, and that's worth protecting.

There's two ways of doing it. You can say, 'The copyright is mine. I will lease it to the publishers to do what they can to promote this song and they will get their cut over a certain period. But the copyright remains mine.' That is the best way of doing it. The other way is saying, 'You have the copyright for three years or whatever,' and, of course, there's an added on period that if they get a hit within those three years, they still collect royalties for the next five sometimes. That's the way it works, so you don't really get your copyright back sometimes for eight years. It gets really complicated and I'm not going to get into it all. But I think that's the first thing: you must ensure that you don't sign away your copyright.

And you must make sure that your deal is a source deal, and that means that when the record's sold in America or the record's sold here or in France or wherever, you get paid when the money is delivered to that particular office. That particular office will pay you directly, not America gets paid, they take their share, then they pay it to the London office, then the London office takes their share, then you get paid. That way you lose half your money.   (GRAHAM LYLE)

GOOD BREAKS

BAD BREAKS

UPS AND DOWNS

I got a gig through a deejay at the Speakeasy club, who saw our band, knew Jackie Lomax was putting a band together and needed a guitar player, and it was just one of those things. So, arguably, if I hadn't ever been slogging round the clubs, I wouldn't have ever got offered the gig. Jackie Lomax at that time was handled by Apple, so suddenly I was whisked into Apple, and I was in there rehearsing every week in the basement, and all kinds of celebrities would be popping in all the time, and occasionally Paul McCartney would come and play the drums. And that was very interesting and it was my introduction to doing sessions.

My first ever session was for Peter and Gordon, their last single, which was a complete flop, I think. So I got a few sessions through Apple and we did some recording with Jackie. Did a tune that Paul McCartney came and produced, then George Harrison did another one.

The union rate, I think, when I first started doing sessions was £9 for three hours on one instrument. If you played two instruments or were required to do lots of tracks, then you'd get paid more. I remember getting my first cheque – £9 per three hours – eighteen quid! Good God! What a life! An Apple pay slip in my hand. (TIM RENWICK)

A band called McGuinness Flint were looking for a bass player, and Benny Gallagher, being the great friend he is, said, 'I'm not coming unless my friend comes along too.' So we both went along that day. I'll never forget it, it was quite amazing, because right away it was great. That first afternoon we were just playing them a few ideas, and pretty quickly we more or less became the writers of the band.

'When I'm Dead And Gone' was one of those ideas we were just messing around with in the afternoon. I didn't even have a guitar with me, I don't think, and Tom McGuinness said, 'Oh, there's a mandolin, have a go on that.' I'd never played a mandolin in my life. I kind of tuned it up and started strumming a few chords and Hughie

Flint started hitting this rhythm on the drums, and I sang any old thing and it sounded great, you know, and we taped a little bit of it and Benny and I took it back home, knocked a song together, and that was it.

It was really instant music. And what was great about it was that we didn't smooth it out, and that roughness was kept in the recording, which often doesn't happen. You start getting clever with it and you smooth out all the edges, and by the time you make the record you've lost the whole spark of what it was about.   (GRAHAM LYLE)

I was very friendly with Dave Courtney and Leo Sayer and all that lot, because they all came from Brighton, and they were looking for a publishing deal, and I'd gone to my boss and said, 'Look, they want publishing. They want sixty thousand quid.' She said, 'You're not in the real world, Neil. People don't pay that kind of money to sign publishing.' And I got really upset and he signed to Chrysalis and was huge, and I thought, 'Oh, I'm moving on. This is too old-fashioned.'   (NEIL FERRIS)

I was in my attic at home and the Stranglers' management company phoned me up and asked me if I'd come and work for them, and I said no. Having made the painful decision to go on my own, I said I wasn't interested, and they asked me to promote the Stranglers' tour, because, although I was essentially a booking agent, I'd actually got back into concert promotion in a small way, which was what a social sec does at university and I was always itching to get back to that area of the business.

It was when the first Stranglers album came out and they agreed to let me promote the whole tour without me having to guarantee them any money. We did a deal whereby we put the tickets on sale and whatever was left after the expenses, we split. In the event the whole tour sold out, the band became huge very quickly, and we all made a fortune. They were very happy, I was very happy.   (PAUL KING)

I'd played on five of Al Stewart's albums, and *The Year Of The Cat* did fantastically well. I remember being very miffed that Al that year was voted Second Best Pop Guitarist in the American *Guitar Player* magazine. I couldn't believe it. They'd just assumed he'd played the guitar on the record.

He paid me a very healthy and handsome sum of money to do the following album, which was way over the top, so that did make up for it to a certain extent, but with a lot of things it's just that pride element, because a lot of people mention the record and you say, 'Oh, I played on that one.' 'Did you? It's my favourite single of all time.' No one seems to know. But I was bitter about that, I must admit, very bitter. I got fifty quid for playing on this thing that sold millions and established his career, and there I am, can't afford to pay my electricity bill, driving around in my Beetle. (TIM REN-WICK)

I bumped into Trevor Horn at a party and he said, 'Could I bring you in a tape?' And I said, 'Yeah, sure.' And he brought it in and played it to me, and I have a very bad memory, but certain images are really stuck in my brain, and I remember we had a long office in the East End of London above a Post Office, opposite Osborn Street where the studio is. And I remember sitting at the desk listening, and I put on the tape and the first track was 'Video Killed The Radio Star', and I remember looking down the room and he was at the other end of the room looking out of the window and I thought, 'My God, this is good! This is very good! This is one of the best things I've heard!' (JILL SINCLAIR)

I got wind of the fact that Virgin were thinking of building a studio in London, so I rang up. Anyway, I got the job before the studios even started, and that was fascinating because we spent six months or so building the Town House. I actually learned how to wire up mike panels and that sort of thing.

Studio 1 was the big studio and halfway through the building of Studio 2, which was going to be the demo studio, they decided that a cheapish 24-track set-up would be the way to go. We'd heard about this new company called SSL and they had a little studio down in Stonesfield near Oxford, and I went down there to check it out one weekend. They'd started building these desks, but they hadn't put one in a commercial studio yet, and we were the first commercial studio in London to have one, and I started working in that studio a lot.

Then I met up with this guy called Steve Lillywhite, who had just started producing. We were both twenty-four, I think, at the time, and he came in with this band – it was XTC – and we immediately hit it off. *Drums And Wires* got an awful lot of critical acclaim and loads of people used to ring up, and I was a staff engineer at the studio, so they used to book me on the sessions, and I used to do virtually all the work in Studio 2, everything from Public Image to reggae bands to other things that I did with Steve, hundreds and hundreds of bands. And the next record, I suppose, was Peter Gabriel's third solo album, which was very important in two ways for my career, because, number one, it was like a really serious Gabriel album. We were really going out there and doing weird things musically and recording, and it was just an incredible experience to go through. I mean, certain technical things that he would want to do that would be like: wow, how do we do that? And I was always a big fan of Genesis when I was at school, so to end up working with Peter Gabriel was like a dream come true. If I never did another job again, my life would be happy, so it was absolutely brilliant doing that.

And then of course the second important thing about that record was that he got Phil Collins to come down and play the drums on two or three tracks. Again we were doing this in Studio 2 at the Town House, so we could get a big drum sound, and it was made even better with Gabriel's record, because he didn't want any cymbals or hi-hat to be played on the record at all, and they were always the ones that messed up the sound limit: when the drummer gets on that ride cymbal, and he's thrashing away on it, it becomes the loudest bit in the room and it was quite difficult to control the sound of it sometimes when recording, so it was like a dream come true, you know. And Phil, I guess, had been the singer in Genesis for four or five years then, but obviously had no solo career, and he must have been impressed because a few months later either he or his manager rang up and said, 'Oh, Phil's written some songs, he's thinking of doing a solo album, he liked what you did on Peter's record, would you like to produce a record with him?'

This is after about two and a half years at the Town House, and Virgin had given me a couple of very minor production things to do, but it was a bit scary, because engineering's one thing, but getting into producing is a totally other thing. But I'd figured through working with some wally producers that, 'God, these guys are really untactful' – or something like this – 'and I know I could do better,' and it was really just from the musical side that I was more apprehensive than anything.

So in a way I was quite glad I'd done a couple of things when Phil had rung up, and I remember going round to his house, it was a really sunny day, and I heard these demos and they sounded great, so we started doing that album and so when that album was successful, suddenly I was a record producer.   (HUGH PADGHAM)

I was with Modern Media five years, and the first year was like the learning stages in actually getting into the front line of promotion. learning how you make sure that people get those records real quick, and I remember with some of the early Pretenders stuff – Gary Crowley used to work there as well, he was like the junior – we used to go round in my car, and we'd actually have phoned the deejays up before, phone Roger Scott at Capital who was doing the afternoon show at the time and phone Peter Powell at Radio 1, and we'd deliver these records in reception, and I remember Roger was on air but would come scuttling down the stairs, grab the record, say, 'When's it out? Where are they?' go scuttling back upstairs, and you're driving away and the record's on the air, and that was so exciting to actually have that radio blasting away with a record he didn't have five minutes ago, and he was getting excited on air about it.   (NIGEL SWEENEY)

I'd worked with Dire Straits for a long time, ever since their inception, and one had seen the building of this, and about that time we were just seeing the launch of CD, and CD was very much going to be one of the selling points of selling a lot of Dire Straits records, and all I did was take a look at what was needed to sell beyond what Dire Straits had ever sold before. They'd had platinum and multi-platinum albums, but we were going into the realms of the unknown, and all I did was draw on all the skills that I think I had as a marketeer and say, 'Well, okay, I've got a great record, I've got a great band, I've got a band going out on tour, who's now reached quite a massive audience, how can I plot this?' Because the band was planning a two-year assault on the world record market, so therefore I should be planning the same kind of assault in marketing terms.

This band was going to start going round the world, but it was going to come back to England, so it was like we could spin the plate – start the plate spinning, then go on and put another one up and another one up and another one up, and when it wobbled at the other end we'd go back and just give it a quick spin, and that's what we did really with *Brothers In Arms*. It was a little bit roller-coastery, we were up and down, but in reality every time it looked like it was going to fall away, we'd most probably look at another single or a bit more TV advertising or we had the promotions with Philips and the CD that we could draw on.

Mark came into the office just after we'd done a million and we went to the little snack bar round the corner from the office and we were talking and he said, 'Well, that's it then, we've sold a million, that's enough, isn't it?' I said, 'What are you talking about?' He said, 'No, I'm quite happy with that, quite happy. Brilliant, isn't it?' I said, 'Well, I think we can do two million.' 'Don't be silly.' And I was biting my lip as I said two million. And, of course, when we got to two million, he was adamant: 'That's quite enough.' But it was a phenomenal thing to be involved in.   (TONY POWELL)

It's a bit like being a junkie, I suppose, because the thrill you get from seeing a group that you've watched from the Kensington (pub) go up and eventually play at Wembley or somewhere like that, it's very gratifying and as long as your ego doesn't get too carried away, you can think, 'Hang on, I had something to do with that.' Or seeing a record climb the charts. That's the most exciting thing. And still every Sunday is the best day of the week really, when you're having a good time, and when you're not, you kick doors and upset the old lady.   (PAUL CONROY)

Paul McGuinness (U2's manager) came and asked us if we were interested in U2, and there was a little bit of pressure to give a quick answer, and we listened to the album for a couple of days, and couldn't get into it, so we said to Paul, 'Look, we're really sorry, we're not really keen,' which now seems like a terrible admission, but nobody really knew them. They'd got a little bit of a live following in Ireland, but nobody really knew them. A lot of record companies had turned them down, a lot of publishing companies had turned them down.

Anyway I kept playing the album in my car and after about a week and a half I'd got into it, and then what happened is I'd gone to Radio 1 for an appointment and it was just sheer chance that I saw Paul McGuinness going past. He was just walking down the street, and I said, 'Come here, come here,' and I turned on the ignition key in the car and the cassette was still on there, and I said, 'It's just brilliant, absolutely brilliant, and we've made a real mistake here,' and he said, 'Right, okay,' and he came back.   (NIGEL SWEENEY)

I was offered Duran Duran during the course of the time I was a promoter in my early career, and I'd paid them fifty quid to support someone in Brighton and they were suddenly asking for £350 and I said, 'No, it's not worth it,' and the next thing I knew they were top of the charts. But that's the luck of the draw. It's a very fast moving business.   (PAUL KING)

Malcolm McLaren came in, and I felt very strongly about Malcolm, and thought it would be interesting to meet him, but I wasn't ever sure about Trevor (Horn) doing the album, but Trevor learned a lot from the album, came out of it with a lot of ideas. Now we don't think anything about it, but the first time I heard 'Buffalo Girls' — people forget now, but we'd never heard anything like that, and the scratchers who did it said, 'How do you scratch on record?' People don't realise the ground that was being broken then. It was very exciting. And I vividly remember the first time I heard 'Buffalo Girls'. I thought it was brilliant. Brilliant. But I suppose I'm Trevor's biggest fan — and his biggest critic.   (JILL SINCLAIR)

There's an open-endedness about press. It can deliver photographs that can be on someone's bedroom wall for months and months and months. It can also formulate better than any other medium an artist's political perspective or what their personal choices are, I think much, much better than televison can, and much, much better than radio can. To me that's always been one of the fascinating things of working in a press office.

There always will be a certain artist that will break through the press. Sade was a classic case in the mid-eighties of somebody that really broke through the amount of press coverage that she had. In fact, Radio 1 were very slow in picking up on 'Your Love Is King' and, if my memory serves me right, they'd only played the record once when it broke into the top 75, but in that week we had already had four covers of the music papers.   (JONATHAN MORRISH)

Touring? The good things? Travel, endless travel. Excitement, great excitement – it's a really good adrenalin-pumping job. Basically getting to go round the world, staying in fabulous hotels, eating in fabulous restaurants, and hopefully going round with a bunch of chums as well. I can't think of another job like it.

The down side? If everything runs as it should do, there isn't really a down side. I really can't think of one.   (PETE BUCKLAND)

The appeal is just working with great characters and great bands. I've turned jobs down just to do a few months with Paul Young, just to hear that voice every night. It's a pleasure to work with a great singer. and if you've got a good team, then it can be a good laugh.   (PAT 'BOILER' LOGUE)

I feel like I've got a job where I've never done a day's work in my life. Every day it's like I'm going off to do my hobby, because I can't think of anything I'd rather do.

But it destroys your social life. You don't really have a social life, because you're working every night. You tend to work very long hours for not much pay, unless you make it and become successful in which case the sky's your limit, you can end up earning a fortune. So you tend to become rather white and unhealthy, unless you're careful to get up in the morning and do exercises. I've learned to some extent the hard way and I'm now quite keen on being fit and stuff like that, but obviously when you're younger you've got more energy and a stronger constitution, so I'd say the down side is that, and it can be quite difficult if you have a home life. Being married and things like that are pretty difficult.

What other down side is there to it? I can't think of any other apart from those really. If there were too many down sides I don't think I'd be doing it. Obviously, I can't say I haven't done albums where I've been thinking, I wish I wasn't doing this, because the artist is being really difficult or making your life hell or it's four o'clock in the morning and you've been up since ten and everyone goes home and the producer who you're working for says, 'Oh, can you do these copies for me?' and that takes two hours. I try not to treat my assistants like that, but I certainly used to be, and some people I'm sure do, so you do end up sometimes with two or three hours' sleep a night, and it can get quite knackering sometimes, but that's often what studio staff are looking for. If you can't handle it, it's no problem for them because they've got a list this long of people who want to come and work there.   (HUGH PADGHAM)

the

· · · · ➤

WAY
IN

TO ENGINEERING AND PRODUCTION . . .

You write letters to the studios. A friend of mine who got into the business at the same time as me in another studio, kept turning up on their doorstep, and he bugged them so much that they gave him a job.

Obviously the business has changed now in that there are many many more studios, but what I did was pick out the top studios, and I kept writing to them. I think what happens, when a job becomes free, is that they tend to look at the letters that have come in that morning, and they do get letters virtually every day for jobs, so I figured that if I just kept writing letters to the same studios every week, when a job became free, my letter would be somewhere in the pile. So I reckon that my best advice would be to get your computer printer now to print the letters out and keep sending them, unless you meet somebody who knows somebody who can ask somebody for you. I think it's the only way really.

I would still advise kids, if they want to end up doing what I do, I still advise them not to go to university, because I really think most of the rock-oriented studios still prefer to train up their own staff. It's an awful thing to say, because a lot of tape ops don't make it to engineer, and a lot of engineers don't make it to producer. The state of the business has changed a lot since I got into it, but I still reckon the best way in is as a tape op at a good studio. That would be my advice. And just keep hassling them until they give you a job. (HUGH PADGHAM)

TO MANAGEMENT . . .

As far as management is concerned, I suppose the only qualification is finding an act, and you can find an act in any number of ways, simply by going out and seeing who's around playing. The other thing in management, of course, is that you're not really being employed, you're not getting into it in the sense of 'Here's my CV – can I have a job?'

If the act is prepared to take you on board, and you're prepared to take them on board, then the next thing is to try and get them onto the roller coaster as it starts up, and that's a rather more complicated thing, and there's no short cut to it. It's a combination of working on the act's talent, getting them exposed wherever you can, doing that awful thing of peddling tapes, ringing up A&R men and trying to get them to come up to Leicester and see them play, and all the rest of it, and I don't really know how that's done any more. I suppose it's all of those things, anything that'll work.

You don't have to be a millionaire to get into music. If you like music and your enthusiasm is there, that's the most important thing. When people say to me, 'I've got a band — what should I do?' I say, 'Give up.' And they look at me agog and say, 'What do you mean?' 'Give up. Pack it in now.' And they laugh nervously and they go, 'I don't want to do that.' And I say, 'Are you sure?' 'Yeah.' 'Well, that's the first battle over.' Because persistence is everything.

And I suppose if there's one thing which most of the people I know who've made it have had in common, once they've found an act that was talented or they could work with, is hard work and what you don't know, ask. Most of the people in my profession, like me, will happily spend time answering questions and so on and so forth, but on the other hand we don't necessarily know the best way.

Interestingly enough, I think most people have a perception that the hardest bit is getting into it. It's not. The hardest bit is when you've had some success and you're trying to hold the whole thing together and you're trying to keep the success going. (ED BICKNELL)

TO THE MUSIC BUSINESS . . .

There is no 'way in'. I suppose my advice would be to do anything that's legal that will get you in. I think the first thing you have to do is you have to accept that you're probably going to have to do it for very little money and a very poor lifestyle to start off with.

Try and get a job in any area that you can, whether it's a roadie, working in a promoter's office, sticking posters on walls, whatever it happens to be. Learn as much as you can, talk to as many people as you can, listen to as many people as you can, read as much as you can, and I don't mean read the charts, which are utter piffle. And choose, of course, the area that you're interested in. Some people are interested in management, some people want to be promoters, some people want to work in record companies, or whatever.

Interestingly enough, record companies and publishers are easier to get into, because they're much more legitimate employment structures. If you buy *Music Week* and scan the ads at the back you'll often see: 'Are you interested in a career in music? Are you twenty-five or younger? Can you drive?' And off you go to EMI to be a sales rep. But any way of getting in is a way of getting in.

And I suppose one of the other things I should say is that socialising is quite an important aspect, because it is a very social business. So there's nothing wrong with spending a bit of time in places where people hang out to meet people. And of course to work hard at your chosen endeavour and to try and make a mark.

The fact that you've got a diploma or a degree from the London College of Design, most people in the pop music business who are in a position to give you work are going to look at it and put it to one side and go, 'So what? What have you done? What can you show me?' So you're peddling your homemade video around — and, after all, if you watch *The Chart Show* every week, there are usually two or three very inexpensive homemade-type clips on that, and I can't stress enough that this idea that you need money and you need power and you need glamour and all the rest of it, the record business is one of the very few truly entrepreneurial things left that anybody can do, because if there's one sure thing in the music industry, nobody has the faintest idea of what's going to do well, not really. What they do know is what *has* done well. Everybody stands exactly the same shot as everybody else at the start point. You are starting in a race where everybody is equal in the sense that nobody has any advantage. You have to make your own advantages.   (ED BICKNELL)

In the old days it was: go to university, go to college, get on the social committee, and then get a job as a booker and the rest is up to you, then you decide what route you want to take. The whole university circuit's disappeared, because, as the amount of equipment bands use has become bigger and bigger, it just physically won't fit into those venues any more. That's all that's happened. People keep asking me, why has that circuit disappeared? It's simply a case of the amount of equipment at the end of the day.

How do you get in now? There's no obvious route. If you're determined and you show that determination to people, they will give you a hearing. If you write to record companies or you phone them up or you write to agencies or you write to promoters, and you convince them that you are serious, they will listen to you.

Getting a job is down to having a sensible CV and determination, that's all it takes really. If you can convince someone that you're serious, they'll give you a shot, and this business, more than probably any other business, is prepared to take on people on a kiss and a prayer, because there are no qualifications. They don't exist.

If I was looking for someone – a member of staff – right now, and some young kid phoned me up and convinced me that he really meant it, I'd give him a shot, but if I got a letter from someone, saying, 'Dear Sir, do you have any vacancies?' it would just go in the filing cabinet with all the rest of them.

I think it's important to be intelligent, but I don't think intelligence is necessarily a direct function of education. Having said that, if you are intelligent, you normally end up having got a good education, but I certainly wouldn't discriminate between a sixteen-year-old having left school and a twenty-one-year-old having left university. In fact, I'd be more suspicious of the twenty-one-year-old than the sixteen-year-old, because if someone goes to university they normally have to pick a subject, so they probably had some route in mind, so why are they at twenty-one suddenly deciding to get into the music business? (PAUL KING)

First of all, don't take no for an answer. Just keep on. There's no point in saying, 'Well, I keep on, but I don't get anywhere,' because this is a business where you have to have lots of guts, you really do.

The best way to get a job in a record company is to find a group that's got a hit and take it to a record company. That's the best best way. People say, 'How do I become a record producer?' Produce a hit record, that's the best way. Produce anything to get experience in any way you can. And nowadays people can do it in their bedrooms. The technology is such that anybody can make a record.

The only rule in the music business is that there are no rules, and any way you can do it, it doesn't matter. If you get in being a secretary, it doesn't matter. There are so many other ways of doing it, from tea boy to temp, it doesn't matter. Get in and learn, and go to gigs and listen to music.

I'm not eighteen any more, but if you are and you're going to clubs, and if you hear something that you think is fabulous and you believe in it, that's the way to do it. That's how all the big managers have made it. Paul McGuinness dedicated his life to U2.

So there are millions of ways of doing it, and there's no point in faltering at the first hurdle or the first lot of rejections that come along, because if you do that you're not meant for the industry anyway, go and join ICI instead, because it's tough, it's very tough. So be out there finding talent. That's what it's about really. Or be talented yourself. Make the record yourself. But don't take no for an answer. Just keep going. And don't lose heart. (JILL SINCLAIR)

TO MUSIC PUBLISHING . . .

The obvious thing is that there's no instant qualification to get started in it. I think you have to be an enthusiast for the music. If you're talking on the creative side, you have to be out there loving the exploration and being a real fan of whatever you're involved in, whether it's limited to a field of music, say, the indie rock scene or the dance scene or whatever. You can't create an interest in it, if it's not naturally there.

People looking to get into the business will probably think about going into agency work or A&R within a record company. Within record companies and increasingly within publishing, promotion is a way in. It means you're enthusiastic about your sort of music, it means that you're actually getting around and meeting a lot of bands and meeting managers and radio and TV people, and also getting a feel for what works.

That could be of value prior to coming into working in publishing. I don't think you can come straight in off the street. You've got to understand how the whole business works a little bit. It's like a taxi driver 'doing the knowledge'. You've got to get an element of the knowledge on board. Nine hundred and ninety-nine times out of a thousand I don't have an opening anyway. Most letters are completely speculative, from people who don't have the knowledge. And my advice to them is usually to do that.

If you are enthusiastic, you've just got to get out on the circuit. There is an established live circuit, be it clubs or be it bands. It's not enough just to go down to the local pub in whatever town it may be or suburb of London it may be, you've actually got to do enough research to find out where the A&R people go, where the publishers go to look at acts, and what acts are they looking at? And that's where to start looking and start forming some opinion, and if you do that you're bound to meet A&R people and publishers, but you've got to have enough nous to find out where the new things are happening. It's not enough to follow the trends, you've actually got to try to find the ones that are going to set the trends before anyone else does. So if you're trying to get a start in the business, you've actually got to get out there and start circulating with the record companies and the publishing companies. They're all out there in these places all the time.

I don't see any real point in sending letters to personnel departments or to managing directors of companies. I think that's trying to hit a bullet with a bullet. It may be interesting just to get some feedback. Hopefully somebody will respond and give you a pointer, but the fact is if you're into music you've got to get out there and get involved with it, get your hands dirty. Nobody's going to say, 'Oh, you're interested in music? I'll help you get your hands dirty.' It's got to come from the individual. I think if you can meet some record company or some publishing people at a junior level, that's the best way to start.   (PAUL CURRAN)

TO PLAYING . . .

I never had music lessons – well, actually I did have piano lessons for a couple of weeks, but I was too young to be interested and I didn't realise I was going to end up making money out of this, so I kick myself. In a way I didn't need them really, just because the interest in the music took the place of lessons, but if I was up and coming I would take lessons, and I'd learn everything I could. Anything you listen to on the radio and you don't understand, get that record and check it out, and find out what it is or ask someone or work it out yourself. Play as much as you can, and with as many kinds of people, because then soon enough you'll know what you really love – it's what you gravitate to. And if you don't make your money making music for yourself, then sessions could be it.

Joining a group is really the best way, because if things don't go well, there's four or five of you you can lean on. You can lean on each other. Just walking up to a studio and saying, 'I'd like to become a session musician,' they'd laugh. It's taken me a lot of years to be asked to do sessions.   (IAN McLAGAN)

TO PUBLIC RELATIONS . . .

It's very difficult to say how to be a PR. You need to get a toe in the water somewhere, and it's always difficult, it's always the chicken and the egg syndrome, but if you're going to go into music PR you do need to have some kind of background in the business, in the music, some kind of understanding of contemporary music, some kind of understanding of journalism, and if you're going to apply for a job in PR with a record company or with an independent, you've got to research the area that you're applying for the job in.

I get an enormous number of applications for jobs that come

through the post at the end of every final year from colleges. You can't do it that way. If it's a record company, you've got to know something about the artists that the record company represents. Go to some trouble to find out who the people are in the company and give some indication that your interest is specifically in this area and you have some specialist knowledge about it.

The academic qualifications in themselves are not really sufficient to attract most employers, they want to know that you have got something a little bit extra. People who apply to me for a job should know who the people are that I represent. That's what you want, that little bit of difference. Research the thing in the same way that you probably would do a project at college or university or whatever. Go into the background of the company or the individual people that you're writing to, like I did when I went for my first job.

Don't make the mistake that seems to be made a lot of the time in this business, that anybody can be a PR. Anybody *can* be a PR, but not necessarily a good one. There is a tendency for anyone that's come out of a social sec situation or something in college or somebody with a second class Bachelor of Arts degree or something to think that they can immediately either become journalists or PRs — and music is something that everybody likes, so they think, 'I'll do that.' It's not like that at all.

Learn how to be a PR. Do something else. Being a journalist to begin with isn't a bad idea, having an appreciation of the people you've got to deal with later.   (KEITH ALTHAM)

TO A RECORD COMPANY . . .

There isn't a this-is-how-you-do-it. Every single story will be different. The only thing that I can say, that I've said to people before, is that you have to be persistent, because there are an awful lot of people who want to get into the music business and a lot of those ones are for the wrong reasons or for reasons which are not strictly correct, which is that it's a very glamorous business, which it isn't.

If you want to get into it, it's important that you impress upon people that you're not getting into it because you think it's glamorous, because nobody will hire you, or very few people will hire you, and anybody that hires you isn't worth the time of day anyway.

Pop stars, generally speaking, are not glamorous. They want to have a cup of tea, they clean their teeth, and they go to the loo like anybody else. They can be charming, they can be ghastly, good, bad and indifferent, like anyone else. They're not very glamorous, and you see the most unglamorous side of them that you can imagine. If it's bad, you'll get it, mostly in the neck.

You've got to seem to be fairly serious about it, that you actually want to work. You've got to be prepared to work very, very hard for not very much money to begin with and you have to keep going back and going, 'I want to do it! I want to do it!' because if you go back to the company six or seven times, it'll irritate them, but at the end of the day they'll go, 'They really are serious, they really do want to get into this.'

But you can't just inundate them, you've got to do it in some sort of an intelligent way, you've got to do it slightly differently each time, have a slightly different approach, write a slightly different letter, be a bit different in your interview, say something that is a bit different each time, but be persistent. But be persistent without carping on about things. That's a very difficult line to tread, but it can be done.

We put an advert in the *Evening Standard* for a secretary one time and about fifty people replied. This young woman was interviewed and they said, 'Oh yes, well you have to come back and be interviewed by the next personnel person.' Instead of going away, she said, 'Will he be back today?' And they said, 'Oh, probably in a couple of hours, three or four hours. Don't stay.' And she said, 'Oh well, I'll just wait in case he will be free.'

Now, he wasn't free when he got back, but she didn't insist on going to see him, and because she had sat there in a very composed manner and read the papers and read a book and read the music papers and was taking an interest in what was going on, helped somebody out at some point – helped lift something or made somebody a cup of tea or whatever it was – she was persistent without being a pain in the arse, and that got noted, so when she came back next day for her second interview, she was already ahead of the game.

She got the job, she became my secretary, she then became an international promotion person, she ended up travelling around the world with Peter Gabriel and various other people and she's a very competent international promotions manager even now as we speak. So she was persistent without being a pain. That's the best advice I can give.   (LISA ANDERSON)

It's hard to get into the music business. The music business has never been what you know, it's who you know. People will come in and bang on my door and I'll say, 'I'm impressed by you. Why don't you learn to be a plugger? Why don't you go off and do this? Why don't you impress me in the building? Come in and do a few days' work during the holidays or something like that?'

The advice I would give somebody is to write a really good letter with a CV, even send a photo in, and you've got almost to beg a bit, say, 'Please give me a chance to come in and talk to you,' but if you send a witty and clever letter in, but concise, those are the people I'll always see, and think, 'Hey, this is a bright spark, I'll give this person a chance to come in.'   (PAUL CONROY)

TO RECORD PROMOTION . . .

What do you do if you decide you want to be a promotion person? Being a sales rep and going through the sales side of things is fairly good training. Or just being in a position where you can be seen to be good dealing with people, because that really is all it is. The bottom line of being a promotion person is you've got to be everybody's mate and you've got to know what you're talking about, you've really got to be interested in what you're doing, you've got to be accurate with your information, have a good grounding in the product, and be able to get on with people, know where you can get things, know how you can make things happen.

It's no use saying, 'What do I do next?' You've got to know that. And many times the only way you can do that is a hands-on approach. I can only speak from my experience, but that's what's happened to me and that's what's happened to the people that have worked for me. I'm very proud that quite a considerable percentage of the people working in promotions at the moment came through me and EMI. One guy, my wife was dealing with him, he was doing freight shipping, and she said you should see this guy, he's great, and he came and saw me, I thought he was great and gave him a job. Another guy we got was a chef, who's now a general manager of one of the other companies. He came to us when he was working in a hotel. There's no set way, but it is the ability to deal with people on lots of different levels and to be a reasonably nice person yourself, not to have any particularly bad habits and to be, not bland, but fairly easy-going and not be given to extremes of behaviour.

It's a hands-on learning experience, it's getting that break to get in there. I can't see there being a college or university course for my job. A major thing is if you can deal with people on a lot of different levels, you've always got something going for you in that way, and you're reliable – it's fairly obvious stuff – then you're on a starter.   (MALCOLM HILL)

TO SONGWRITING . . .

The traditional way in this country is to form a band, to be part of a band, or even if it's just two of you, you know, then it becomes a more marketable thing, as far as the business is concerned, then they've got two bites at the cherry. The business thinks, 'Well, okay, they write good stuff, but they could make records too, so we can not only make on the performance of the songs, we can actually sell records and make on the mechanical side of it. Plus, if they get a deal, we've got guaranteed ten tracks or whatever it is on an album out there in the market place. If they've got a deal, we've got a guarantee probably of two, maybe three singles.'

And even if a song isn't a hit, if it gets a fair amount of air play then the publishers are making money, so if a publisher can't visualise promoting the songs for the songs' sake, just purely doing what I'm doing, he may take on the writer or writers with the idea of going out themselves and getting a deal with a record company – that's becoming more popular, because what happens is the publisher has very little outlay in business terms. If he can get a record company interested, the record company has the outlay really, because it costs so much to make an album, which the publisher doesn't have to contribute to at all. He obviously has to pay the writer some advance, but with a new writer that can be as little as a grand, two grand, fifteen hundred, so sometimes it makes a lot of sense to them to approach it in that way.

I think it's extremely difficult for a writer in Britain, without having any deal before, to expect to be signed as a writer of songs and nothing else. My advice would be to try and form a band. It also helps with the writing, because I know, having played to live audiences and done tours, that it makes you a stronger writer, it makes you realise the sort of songs that actually connect to people, and that's something that you can't really learn sitting in a room, you can't really learn that. It's communication. It teaches you about lyrics. A lyric communicates to a live audience in a way that you'd never realised when you wrote the record. The record to you was: well, it sounded like a hit, it had that sound about it, that exciting sound. You didn't really think the lyrics had much to do with it. But when you go out and play to an audience, you realise how much these lyrics had meant to people, and they come up and they tell you – 'You know that really meant something to me and my girlfriend' or whatever – and then it suddenly makes sense.

Without a reputation you won't get the artist coming to you, you won't get an A&R person coming to you, and realistically that is one of the few ways you will get a fair listening for your song, if they have requested it in the first place. It still doesn't guarantee a reaction, but there's obviously a better chance of it.

So what you're doing is sending out tapes blind and nowadays, especially in America, sometimes they won't even open the tape. They call it 'unsolicited material', they're scared of being sued. I don't want to be negative about this, but that is a fact: for a writer to send his best song, something that he's spent maybe six months working over, to Whitney Houston, he can hear it being a No 1, it's a waste of time. It won't even be opened. So you've got to be with a publisher who has access to these people. That's the first thing. Then there's a chance that your song will get a fair listening. It still is not guaranteed, because everybody in the world thinks they can write a song, and everybody in the world probably *can* write a song, so these people get so many tapes in, if they do play it, it has to hit them within the first fifteen to twenty seconds that this is worth continuing with.

Obviously you gain a reputation, and with a reputation there's a better chance of getting paid attention to, and artists come to you, rather than you trying to run after them – that's the big plus – but the bottom line is you've still got to deliver a hit record. That's the way I approach it.　(GRAHAM LYLE)

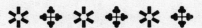

APPENDIX

APPENDIX

Besides the British Recording Industry Trust School for the Performing Arts and Technology, 60 The Crescent, Croydon CR0 2HN (081 665 5242), which opened in September 1991, the following institutes of education offer music courses:

Aberdeen College of Commerce
Tel: 0224 572811
(National Certificate Programme in Music Studies/Licentiate of Trinity College London Diploma Courses)

Accrington & Rossendale College
Tel: 0254 35334
(Lancashire Music Foundation Diploma)

Bath College of Higher Education
Tel: 0225 873701
(Diploma of Higher Education)

Belfast Queens University
Tel: 0232 245133
(Extra-mural Certificate in Music)

Birmingham Polytechnic
Tel: 021 331 5000
(Graduate of the Birmingham School of Music)

Blackpool & Fylde College
Tel: 0253 52352
(Music Foundation Certificate)

Boston College of Further Education
Tel: 0205 65701
(Music with GCSE or A levels)
Bournemouth & Poole College of Art & Design
Tel: 0202 533011
(College Certificate in Music)
Bournemouth & Poole College of Further Education
Tel: 0202 747600
(Main Music Course/Advanced Music
Theory & Diploma Preparation)
Bromsgrove College of Further Education
Tel: 0527 79500
(Music Foundation Course/Diploma
in Music Theory)
Cauldon College of Further Education
Tel: 0782 29561
(Music Diploma for Teachers,
Accompanists & Performers)
Chichester College of Technology
Tel: 0243 786321
(College Diploma in Music)
Clarendon College of Further Education
Tel: 0602 607201
(Music Preliminary with A levels/Music Diploma)
Cleveland Technical College
Tel: 0642 473132
(Diploma in Music/Graded Theory of Music)
Colchester Institute
Tel: 0206 761660
(Graduate Diploma in Music/External Diploma
in Music/Foundation Course in Music)

Crewe & Alsager College of Higher Education
Tel: 0270 500661
(DipHE/BA Hons Combined Studies)
Cricklade College
Tel: 0264 63311
(Pre-Professional Music Courses)
Derby College of Further Education
Tel: 0332 573012
(Light Music)
Doncaster Institute of Higher Education
Tel: 0302 22122
(Diploma/Pre-Diploma in Music)
Durham New College
Tel: 091 386 2421
(Certificate/Advanced Certificate
in Light Music/HND Business Studies, Music &
Entertainment)
Filton Technical College
Tel: 0303 862224
(Foundation Music)
Handsworth Technical College
Tel: 021 551 6031
(Music Industry Training)
Harrogate College of Art & Technology
Tel: 0423 55631
(Foundation Certificate in Music)
uddersfield Polytechnic
Tel: 0484 22288
(Polytechnic Graduate Diploma in Music)

Huddersfield Technical College
Tel: 0484 36521
(Preparatory Course in Music/Diploma
in Music/External Diploma in Music)
James Watt College
Tel: 0475 24433
(National Certificate Programme
in Sound & Music Management)
Jewel & Esk Valley College
Tel: 031 663 1951
(National Certificate Programme
in Practical Music)
Kingsway Princeton College
Tel: 071 278 0541
(Young Musicians Course/General Muscianship)
Lancashire Polytechnic
Tel: 0772 22141
(Foundation Course in Music)
Leeds College of Music
Tel: 0532 452069
(Graduate Diploma
in Jazz & Contemporary Music/Diploma
in Music/Foundation Certificate in Music/Music
Elementary, Intermediate
or Advanced Certificate)
Leigh College
Tel: 0942 608811
(Foundation/Pre-Foundation Course
in Light Music)

London College of Music
Tel: 071 437 6120
(Graduate Course in Music)
City of London Polytechnic
Tel: 071 481 2774/2095
(HND Musical Instrument Technology)
Central Manchester College
Tel: 061 223 8282
(First Diploma in Music Technology)
North Manchester Community College
Tel: 061 740 1491
(Foundation Course in Music)
Middlesex Polytechnic
Tel: 081 368 1299
(BA Hons in Contemporary Cultural Studies)
Neath College
Tel: 0639 54271
(Music Diploma)
Nelson & Colne College
Tel: 0282 603151
(Lancashire Music Foundation Course)
Nene College
Tel: 0244 817531
(BA Hons/BSc Hons in Combined Studies)
Newark Technical College
Tel: 0636 705921
(Music Preparatory)
Newcastle College of Arts & Technology
Tel: 0632 738866
(Graduate Diploma in Music/Preparatory Course in Music
and/or Performing Arts/Foundation Course in Music

North Herts College
Tel: 0462 32351/2/3
(Preparatory Music Certificate or Diploma)
North Warwickshire College of Technology & Art
Tel: 0203 349321
(Warwickshire County Music Course Preparatory or
Foundation Level)
Oldham College of Technology
Tel: 061 624 5214
(Foundation Course in Music)
Oxford Polytechnic
Tel: 0865 741111
(BA/BA Hons; BSc/BSc Hons; BEd Hons)
Peterborough Technical College
Tel: 0733 67366
(Foundation Course in Music)
Pontypool College
Tel: 0495 755141
(Foundation Course in Music & Drama)
Rotherham College of Art, Science and Technology
Tel: 0709 62111
(Preparatory Course in Music)
Royal Academy of Music
Tel: 071 935 5461
(Graduate Royal Schools of Music Hons)
Royal College of Music
Tel: 071 589 3643
(Graduate Royal Schools of Music Hons)
Royal Northern College of Music
Tel: 061 273 6283
(Graduate Northern College of Music)

Royal Scottish Academy of Music & Drama
Tel: 041 332 4101
(Diploma of Royal Scottish Academy
of Music & Dance/Improved Standard
of Performance)
Salford College of Technology
Tel: 061 736 6541
(Higher College Diploma in Popular
Music with Recording/Higher National Diploma in
Performing Arts)
Sandown College
Tel: 051 254 1239
(Graduate Diploma in Music/Diploma in Light
Music/Certificate in Rock Music)
South Cheshire College
Tel: 0270 69133
(Preliminary Light Music Certificate)
South Downs College of Further Education
Tel: 0705 257011
(Music Diploma)
Southend College of Technology
Tel: 0702 353931
(Music Diplomas)
Stockton & Billingham Technical College
Tel: 0642 552101
(Diploma in Music/Foundation Course
in Music/Continuation Course in Music Theory)
Sunderland Polytechnic
Tel: 091 567 6231
(Diploma in Music)

Tameside College of Technology
Tel: 061 330 6911
(National Diploma in Performing Arts)
Trinity College of Music
Tel: 071 935 5773
(Diploma of Graduate of Trinity College of Music)
Ulster University
Tel: 0265 44141
(Certificate in Foundation Studies in Music)
Wakefield District College
Tel: 0924 370501
(Foundation Diploma in LIght Music)
Welsh College of Music & Drama
Tel: 0222 342854
(Performers Course/Advanced
Certificate Course in Music)
West Kent College of Further Education
Tel: 0732 358101
(Diploma in Music)
West London Institute
Tel: 081 891 0121
(Foundation Course in Music/Diploma in Music)
West Lothian College of Further Education
Tel: 0506 634300
(Higher National Certificate in Business Studies/Music
Management option)
Wolverhampton Polytechnic
Tel: 0902 313001
(Diploma/Diploma Hons in Musicianship)

WILLIAM GILMOUR

THE CLUB: HELLO, AMERICA!

If your brother died on tour, would you join the same band?

John nearly hadn't auditioned but now here he was on his way to America, the new guitarist for The Messengers. The playing side he could do easily. But could he keep his identity a secret? And would he be able to find out how his brother really died?

Hello, America! We're back . . .

WILLIAM GILMOUR

THE CLUB: ALL THE WAY FROM MEMPHIS

Jan adjusted the height of the microphone to her mouth and kept hold of the stand. She hung on, aware of the extra heat from the lights above her head, focussing on the wall furthest from her to hold the room steady and turn the staring faces in front of her into a blur.

Feeling the music lift her into song she gave the first two verses a slow build, holding back, letting the dynamics establish naturally. Now she was thinking of John, singing those words for him, and she started to scan the faces in front of her, as if he was still around, as if it had all been a bad dream, and he was going to come out of the crowd at the end and hug her . . .

The second book in *The Club* series.

WILLIAM GILMOUR

THE CLUB: DON'T PLAY THAT SONG

Playing on a small stage in The Cellar definitely isn't the Big Time, but to John and the rest of the band it's knowing that if they are ever going to make it, it would be because of this place and their faithful fans.

Shirley from Round Records knows The Club could reach the top but her boss, Dick Robbins, sees things differently. Determined to help the group, Shirley gives rival Aurora Records the tip-off. Suddenly the race to sign The Club is on . . .

The third book in *The Club* series.